FATHERS IN JANE AUSTEN

The role of fathers and father figures in Jane Austen's novels,
showing how the destiny of the daughter is dependent
upon the father's character and foibles

by

I P DUCKFIELD

To George.
For your Birthday
on 2nd August 2017.
Irene Duckfield.
July 2017

The moral right of the author has been asserted in accordance with the Copyright, Designs and Patents Act 1988.

All rights reserved. No part of this e-book publication may be reproduced, stored in a retrieval system, or transmitted, in any form or by any means, without the prior written permission of the author, nor be otherwise circulated in any form of binding or cover other than that in which it is published and without a similar condition being imposed on the subsequent purchaser.
This e-book is licensed for your personal enjoyment only. Please purchase subsequent copies if you wish to share it with others. Thank you for respecting the work of this author.

Kindle Edition 2015

Copyright © I P Duckfield 2015

For readers of Jane Austen's novels

CONTENTS

	Introduction	1
1.	Mr Bennet: the complete delinquent	17
2.	Mr Woodhouse: the complete dependant	41
3.	Mr Morland: a good father, and General Tilney: the complete tyrant	63
4.	Sir Walter Elliot: the witless peacock	87
5.	Sir Thomas Bertram: a tragic figure	101
6.	Orphans and Outsourcing	129
	Conclusion	153

Author's Note: All references to the novels are to the Penguin English Library paperback edition of 2012. Citations are given in brackets in the body of the text, taking the form of the initials of the title (e.g. *MP* for *Mansfield Park*) followed by the volume, chapter and page number/s.

INTRODUCTION

The novels of Jane Austen (1775–1817) are typically regarded as romantic comedies in which the heroine overcomes the obstacles that stand between her and a "happy ever after" life with the hero. What is not usually observed is that the obstacles have been created by the heroines' fathers or by other important father figures in their lives. The fathers hold the key to the novels and to the destinies of the daughters. They represent power and authority within their families. How the fathers use their power and authority gives impetus to the story. The narratives derive from the fathers' failures, misjudgements and neglect. They create difficulties which impair the daughters' happiness and their marriage prospects. Instead of promoting the daughters' chances of happy marriages, the fathers in these novels represent the biggest threats to it. Whether indifferent, cruel, selfish, withdrawn, stupid, spendthrift or emotionally cold, Austen's novels provide a catalogue of the mistakes a father can make and a description of the damage he can cause.

The heroines are trapped by their fathers' characters and actions. The point of the novels is to create the circumstances under which they can escape. This is where the heroes come in – where there are heroes. Not all the novels have a hero who takes the form of the heroine's love interest, although some do (in *Pride and Prejudice* (1813), *Emma* (1815) and *Persuasion* (published posthumously in 1818)). In *Sense and Sensibility* (1811) and *Mansfield Park* (1814), the male love interests (Edward Ferrars, and Edmund Bertram, respectively) are not equal to the task, while the role of liberator is played by Colonel Brandon in *Sense and Sensibility* and by the heroine herself (Fanny Price) in *Mansfield Park*. Henry Tilney, the hero of *Northanger Abbey* (published posthumously in 1818), does not have the power to release himself and Catherine Morland from his father's cruel and capricious behaviour, and has to await a lucky death to unlock his father's opposition. The role of the hero, where it exists, is to neutralise the adverse effects of the father's character or behaviour, or to fill a vacuum left by the father, thereby achieving a transition for the heroine from chaos and unhappiness to order and tranquillity. This must be accomplished without causing a family rift and without overstepping the bounds of propriety. Heroes and heroines alike must bear any self-sacrifice with true stoicism. Their reward is the prospect of a life of happiness and fulfilment with each other.

In the journey from imprisonment to freedom, not all the daughters are liberated, and not all end up with the ideal husband. Austen's books are littered with daughters who do not achieve a triumphant transformation, with or without a hero. Some are left stranded or exiled, perpetually damaged by their fathers' inadequacies and errors. Others opt for the first available man who will have them, rather than hold out for a romantic partner. Austen concentrates on the principal characters' success in overcoming obstacles to achieve love's young dream, but she is realistic enough to include examples of the mundane and the tragic. She believes the fathers are at the bottom of it all.

In the chapters that follow, Austen's fathers, whether natural fathers or appointed guardians, will be measured against a set of three simple standards by which Austen assesses the fathers she creates: the provision of financial security, of education, and of moral principles. All will be found wanting, especially when it comes to providing good moral values. However rich and well tutored, the daughters fall furthest where principle is lacking. It will be shown that the fathers' failures to meet one or more of the three standards result in the heroines' personal and romantic difficulties.

The first and basic duty of a father, as presented by Austen, is to provide a financially secure and harmonious home, and to ensure that, in the event of his death, his family will not be destitute. Some of her fathers fall at this first fence. Success in this first duty depends to a large extent upon choosing the right wife. The principal fathers in the novels have either chosen an unsuitable wife or their wives have died young. Either way, the fathers are in a position analogous to single parents when it comes to bringing up their children. They make their own decisions.

Whether husband or widower, no home is secure unless the family lives within its means. Austen is very strict about this. Money looms large in these novels: having it, lacking it, spending it whether you have it or not, being mean about it, money as a lure or a weapon, especially in marriage. Money is power. It provides security. It makes the daughters more marriageable. Austen does not underestimate the importance of money. She does not let her worthy characters marry where they do not have enough of it, but she is dead against money as a motive for marriage. She is also conscious that life is uncertain. A husband's failure to make provision for the family in the event of his death is another breach of his financial duty towards them. Austen's fathers are either neglectful or venal. Three of her fathers are improvident: Mr Bennet in *Pride and Prejudice*, Sir Walter Elliot in *Persuasion*, and Mr Dashwood in *Sense and Sensibility*. In each case, the father's negligence in matters of money has an important bearing on the story and on the predicament of the daughters. Where the fathers are wealthy (Mr Woodhouse in *Emma*, Sir Thomas Bertram in *Mansfield Park*, and General Tilney in *Northanger Abbey*), they do not use their wealth to promote the happiness of their daughters.

The second practical benefit a father must provide for his daughters is education. Education extends from the usual subjects such as literature, history, geography, foreign languages and mathematics, to proficiency in music and drawing, and to manners or etiquette. Again, the record of the Austen fathers is mixed, ranging from them being outright neglectful to overly strict. General Tilney in *Northanger Abbey*, Sir Thomas Bertram in *Mansfield Park* and Mr Dashwood in *Sense and Sensibility* score highly on formal education. Mr Woodhouse in *Emma* thinks he has done well, but he fails in a way that enhances the flaws in Emma's character. Sir Walter Elliot in *Persuasion*, no intellectual himself, does not really bother. Mr Bennet, in *Pride and Prejudice*, despite being very bookish, does absolutely nothing about it. Instead, he makes a parade of his younger daughters' silliness and mocks them for it.

Education is not provided so that the daughters can earn a living (Jane Fairfax in *Emma* apart), but so that they can develop their minds and moral principles, become socially confident and engaging, and cultivate elegance and taste. These accomplishments will develop their intellect and powers of conversation, help them enjoy their lives, and, crucially, serve them well in the marriage market as they compete with other women for eligible men. Most entertainment in the novels is conducted within the home, with or without neighbours present: conversation, drawing, cards, playing musical instruments, singing, and reading. Being a good performer is important in Austen's world, and supplies a means of occupying the large amount of leisure time the families all enjoyed. The women are also well aware of the advantages of performing well in attracting men, as Mary Crawford shows in *Mansfield Park*. She makes special arrangements to bring her harp up from London and entrances Edmund Bertram with her playing. Neglecting the development of these accomplishments was therefore not in the interests of the daughters.

The third aspect is the respectability, happiness and well-being that comes with a strong sense of right and wrong, and with self-denial. There must be a genuine, heartfelt wish on the part of the father to make his daughter happy, and to secure the ultimately precious status of respectability. Once respectability is lost it is irretrievable, and the daughter is cast into a social wilderness, taking her family with her. The father must therefore protect his daughter from harm, whether physical or moral. He should vet her choice of friends and, particularly, her choice of husband. He should watch how she conducts herself towards others, and step in when guidance is needed. A father should be a good communicator about all this, forming a close relationship of mutual confidence, affection and trust. All the principal fathers make a complete mess of this aspect of their role.

Austen also expects her fathers to achieve a balance between the three formal aspects of the paternal role (providing financial security, education and moral guidance), with the softer qualities of love, concern, affection, and kindness. A father must have good judgement as to what is best for his daughter as opposed to what she wants. He should make a stand in favour of principle, even if this means disappointment for the daughter. Mr Morland does this when he refuses to consent to Catherine's marriage to Henry Tilney in *Northanger Abbey* because General Tilney is opposed to it. A father should not be indulgent – at least not often; that is for mothers. A mother who indulges her daughter without the restraint of a father's authority puts the daughters at great risk, and there are several examples of such mothers in the novels (Mrs Dashwood and Lady Middleton in *Sense and Sensibility*, Mrs Bennet in *Pride and Prejudice*, Lady Bertram in *Mansfield Park*, Mrs Thorpe in *Northanger Abbey*). There is also one father who does this: Mr Woodhouse in *Emma*. It is the father's role to act as a counterweight to this maternal tendency to indulgence, and to intervene where necessary. Although Austen depicts so many indolent and indulgent mothers, it is the fathers whom she holds responsible for the consequences.

Being a father is not a popularity contest. He must be prepared to incur disapproval when exerting authority in the best interests of the family. He is not expected to shirk his moral responsibility in order to avoid awkwardness, tension or resentment. Sir Thomas Bertram shirks his responsibility in *Mansfield Park* when he puts up only mild opposition to his elder daughter Maria's marriage to Rushworth. A successful father will not, however, have to worry about being unpopular, or not for long. He will have shared his values and principles with his family. While his daughter may not like his decision, she understands the reason behind it. She knows that he is emotionally committed to her. His motives will be clear, and his character and principles respected. He should be a benign enforcer, but an enforcer nonetheless. No one said this was going to be easy, but the penalties for a father's failure are severe from the daughter's point of view. All Austen's principal fathers, and many of the minor fathers, fail in the third duty of imparting good moral standards. This is the essence of their role in the novels. If they were competent fathers, there would be no story.

The catalogue of qualifications and behaviours that a good father must have and deploy resembles Mr Darcy's description, in *Pride and Prejudice*, of accomplished women. He says he knows no more than six of them and then lists the many talents they must possess to qualify as accomplished. Elizabeth retorts: "I am no longer surprised at your knowing *only* six accomplished women. I rather wonder now at your knowing *any*" (*PP* I.8.39).

There are just two characters in the novels who buck the trend and are definitely good fathers. A few other minor characters would likely also pass the tests, but their role as fathers is not important. The good fathers are also good husbands, who have married sensibly and share a moral outlook with their wives. They take a joint stand on any issue.

Austen has no interest in well-regulated families, since they make for a dull story, but in passing she does describe how the good parents act. They may play relatively minor roles as far as the action is concerned, but they provide reminders of how Austen expects fathers to behave and serve to highlight the failings of the others.

The comical behaviour and eccentricities of the incompetent fathers distract the reader from the profoundly destructive impact they have, or come close to having. Their daughters are at risk of losing some or all of their respectability, prosperity and happiness, either blighting their lives, or coming within a hair's breadth of doing so. The adverse effects of a delinquent or incompetent father fall mainly on the daughters, but sons are not immune. This is the case for Henry Tilney in *Northanger Abbey*, in which General Tilney is the obstacle to happiness, not Mr Morland, father of the heroine. In *Mansfield Park*, Sir Thomas Bertram's sons suffer too, although not in the same way as his daughters and Fanny Price, his adopted niece.

Sometimes the heroine's selection of husband is directed by a need to fill the vacuum left by the father (Darcy in *Pride and Prejudice*, Mr Knightley in *Emma*, Edmund in *Mansfield Park*). Austen's principal characters escape so that there can be a happy ending, but the books are not short of examples of daughters (and some sons) permanently damaged by their fathers. So Lady Catherine de Bourgh may be of the view that "Daughters are never of so much consequence to a father" (*PP* II.14.213), but in cases where that is portrayed in the novels, Austen shows that she deplores it and demonstrates how miserable it can make both father and daughter.

Before considering the fathers in detail, there are two general points to make about the differences between the circumstances depicted in the novels, set in the late eighteenth and early nineteenth centuries, and those of the twenty-first century. One is the value of money and the characters' source of income. Whether or not characters have money and how much of it they have are matters often of great importance to Austen's plots. According to the Bank of England's online calculator (which goes back to 1750), £1,000 in Austen's day would be the equivalent of £66,500 in 2012. There was no income tax. Government securities yielded between 3% and 5%. So, by this measure, Bingley in *Pride and Prejudice*, left £100,000 by his father, would be worth around £7 million today, and his annual income would be about a quarter of a million pounds. Rushworth in *Mansfield Park* has £12,000 a year, the equivalent of £800,000 today. These are not exact comparisons, but it gives some idea to the modern reader of how well or badly off the characters are. Approximate modern equivalents of the figures mentioned, calculated on this basis, are included in the text.

Around the turn of the nineteenth century, there was absolutely no social security net. If you had no money, then you were destitute, out on the streets if your family could not or would not step in. Women, with so little opportunity for employment, were particularly vulnerable. Their vulnerability sharpened their competitiveness when it came to marriage. Men, especially younger sons, had to look for employment if the family provision was not adequate. This may have been because the family did not want to split any land, keeping it intact and leaving it solely to the elder son (for example, the

Knightley brothers in *Emma*, the Tilney brothers in *Northanger Abbey*, Darcy's cousin Colonel Fitzwilliam in *Pride and Prejudice*). The navy, the army and the Church were the most popular employments for younger sons, although John Knightley, younger brother of Mr Knightley in *Emma*, goes into the law. The military offered the spoils of war against the French, and the consequent acceleration up the economic and social scale, a rise deplored by Sir Walter Elliot in *Persuasion*, snob that he is. The Church offered "livings". A living was a fixed income derived from Church property and attached to a particular parish. The vicar was meant to live on that income. In some cases the income from the living was too low to support him or to support a family, so some clergymen held more than one. Livings were often in the gift of a local landowner. In *Pride and Prejudice* Mr and Mrs Collins are assiduous in their courtesies towards Lady Catherine as a "patron", because she probably had more livings in her gift than the one she has already granted. When Mr Bennet recommends to Mr Collins that he should take Darcy's side against Lady Catherine in the row over Darcy's engagement to Elizabeth, he offers the cynical advice: "Console Lady Catherine as well as you can. But, if I were you, I would stand by [Darcy]. He has more to give" (*PP* III.18.384). This is a reference to Darcy likely having more livings in his gift than his aunt.

The second, less measurable, aspect of life in Austen's day is the degree of disgrace brought on by an elopement without marriage amongst the well-to-do classes. Cohabitation was a sin. Sex outside marriage was a vice. Pregnancy outside marriage stigmatised a woman for life. It was therefore vital that girls were taught to control their emotions to avoid succumbing to sexual temptation. In *Pride and Prejudice*, after

Lydia and Wickham have eloped, Elizabeth Bennet reflects: "how little of permanent happiness could belong to a couple who were only brought together because their passions were stronger than their virtue" (*PP* III.8.313). This is the nub of it. Sexual attraction is natural and powerful, but giving in to it without the formal trappings of marriage is the short route to losing reputation, respectability and the prospect of long-term happiness with the right partner.

It is hard to comprehend how disgraceful it was for a respectable family if a daughter eloped, was seduced, or cohabited outside marriage. Protecting daughters was vital. As Austen makes very clear, the disgrace affects not just the errant couple, principally the woman, but also both their wider families. It is contaminating. It is difficult to think of a modern equivalent; it might be akin to having a close relative in jail for some appalling offence.

It follows that one of the objectives of parenthood in Jane Austen's day was to protect vulnerable daughters from the temptation of predatory men. There are three elopements in the novels which do not have marriage as the couple's joint objective (although it might have been the woman's intention): the first is Lydia Bennet and Wickham in *Pride and Prejudice*; the second is Mr Elliot's flight with Mrs Clay in *Persuasion*; and the third is Maria Rushworth and Henry Crawford in *Mansfield Park*. In a fourth elopement, that of Julia Bertram and Yates, also in *Mansfield Park*, they intend to and do marry. Wickham's attempt to elope with Darcy's sister in *Pride and Prejudice* is discovered and prevented. Respectability and reputation are hard won, but can be lost in a moment's weakness. In the cases of Lydia, Maria and Julia, it is their fathers' fault that matters come to such a disgraceful pass.

Fathers in Jane Austen

❧

Before embarking on a survey of the fathers in order to show that they have a critical role to play, it is worth setting out a short summary of the territory.

The six fathers who are unimportant in a paternal capacity are: John Knightley in *Emma*, brother of George and married to Emma's older sister Isabella; Sir William Lucas, father of Charlotte in *Pride and Prejudice*; Captain Harville, friend and fellow naval officer of Captain Wentworth in *Persuasion*; Mr Gardiner, Mrs Bennet's brother in *Pride and Prejudice*; John Dashwood in *Sense and Sensibility*; and Colonel Campbell, who assumes responsibility for Jane Fairfax's education and upbringing in *Emma*. Each has a role, and quite an important one in the case of Mr Gardiner, but not as fathers. They are described as probably good fathers for various reasons. John Knightley is clearly in the pipe-and-slippers category, described as liking his home comforts and resenting the Westons' invitation to dinner at Christmas when he and his family are staying at Hartfield with Mr Woodhouse and Emma. He is impatient with Mr Woodhouse, but he is a successful lawyer, astute about other people and actively engaged with his five young children. Not much is likely to go awry here.

Sir William Lucas in *Pride and Prejudice* is a cardboard cut-out: pompous and well-meaning, and highly delighted (as well he might be) with his elder daughter Charlotte's good fortune in snagging Mr Collins. Charlotte, older than Elizabeth Bennet and very plain in looks, has reached the age where her unmarried status is beginning to become an embarrassment to herself and her family, a dent in Sir William's self-esteem. An intelligent woman, she opportunistically creates her own escape, exchanging a narrow home life for the security of her own establishment, notwithstanding the unattractive nature – intellectually and physically – of her husband. She is in the category of taking the first available man. Indeed, she seeks him out especially for the purpose once her friend Elizabeth has rejected him, realising that romance is not in his DNA and that any wife will do for him. Sir William makes one other contribution to the development of the story: his indiscreet hints during the Netherfield ball tip off Darcy that there is a general expectation in Meryton of Bingley marrying Jane Bennet. Darcy reacts by taking Bingley to London, out of the way of such an unsuitable alliance.

In *Persuasion* Captain Harville, a friend of Captain Wentworth and a resident of Lyme, gives houseroom to Captain Benwick, formerly engaged to Harville's late sister. He is important as the magnet for the trip to Lyme where the famous accident occurs. He has children who are barely referred to, but he is clearly a good egg, and his children are not likely to go astray.

Mr Gardiner is the most important of the also-rans. He plays several significant roles in *Pride and Prejudice*: he and his wife are instrumental in taking Elizabeth into Derbyshire; he shows Darcy that Elizabeth has some well-bred and intelligent relations for whom she need not blush; and he relieves Mr Bennet of the strain of seeking out Lydia and Wickham, eventually conspiring with Darcy to arrange their marriage. The Gardiners have children, but they are not much in evidence. As with all the acceptable couples, he and Mrs Gardiner are very much an item and there can be no doubt that their children are being brought up in accordance with Austen's approved approach; we would hear more about them if they were not.

John Dashwood in *Sense and Sensibility* is an unpleasant character and has married an entirely compatible wife. He reneges on a promise given to his father on his death bed and wriggles out of supporting his step-mother and three half-sisters. He has a son, but it is his behaviour as a son himself, rather than as a father, which is of importance.

Finally, Colonel Campbell in *Emma*, who never appears and is only ever described by others, is a friend of Jane Fairfax's late father. Jane is an orphan, and niece to Miss Bates. Colonel Campbell assumes responsibility for her education and upbringing. Not being rich enough to provide a capital sum for both his own daughter and for her, he educates Jane to earn her living as a governess. He is described in glowing terms, but he is important only to provide an explanation for Jane Fairfax's predicament as a woman of great refinement and taste, but no money.

The only two fathers who are expressly held up as model fathers are Mr Morland in *Northanger Abbey* and the senior Mr Musgrove in *Persuasion*. They have modest parts overall, reflecting Austen's relentless focus on the dysfunctional. In considering Mr Morland, Mr Allen, the Morlands' wealthier and childless neighbour will be discussed in more detail in Chapter 3 on General Tilney. The senior Mr Musgrove is considered in Chapter 4.

Before describing those many fathers who more or less make a hash of it, and provide the plotline in the process, there are three who send out distress signals of trouble to come. They are Charles Musgrove junior in *Persuasion*, and Sir John Middleton and Mr Palmer, both in *Sense and Sensibility*. Austen tells us enough about what she sees as the symptoms of poor fatherhood for the reader to see it coming. These three relatively minor characters are radiating signs of failure, largely as a result of marrying the wrong women.

Charles Musgrove has married Mary, the youngest of the Elliot daughters. In so doing, he has had the unfortunate experience of having to marry his second choice. He preferred Anne, but had to settle for her querulous sister Mary. In a small neighbourhood, where choice is limited, he has been pragmatic. His two eldest sisters cheerfully tell Captain Wentworth that they would have much preferred Anne, and Charles would no doubt agree with them. He has married a less than congenial woman, and prefers outdoor sports to the domestic hearth. This relative lack of suitability comes out in Charles's and Mary's attitudes to their two boisterous, out-of-control boys, whom their mother does not attempt to discipline, as she seems to possess neither the knack nor the interest – perhaps the two go together. Charles does better than she does. Austen comments: "As to the management of their children, his theory was much better than his wife's and his practice not so bad" (*P* I.6.43). But his inability to adopt a consistent approach in active co-operation with Mary, and his relative lack of application to a thankless task bode ill for the little Musgroves in later life.

Sir John Middleton, a distant relation of the Dashwood family, becomes a benefactor to the widow Dashwood and her three daughters in *Sense and Sensibility*. He offers Mrs Dashwood an affordable means of escape from the tensions of her cohabitation at Norland Park with Mr and Mrs John Dashwood, her stepson and his wife. The move to Barton Cottage in Devonshire shifts the action and brings into the story various characters of importance: Colonel Brandon, Willoughby, and the Steele sisters. Sir John's four children are as spoiled as Charles Musgrove's and their mother is equally disinterested. The Steele sisters fuss over the children as a means of ingratiating themselves with Lady Middleton. Lucy Steele observes to Elinor Dashwood: "I have a notion ... you think the little Middletons rather too much indulged ... I cannot bear [children] if they are tame and quiet" (*SS* I.21.120). To which Elinor replies: "I confess ... that while I am at Barton Park, I never think of tame and quiet children with any abhorrence" (*SS* I.21.121). This benign neglect bodes ill for the children's future, but it is Sir John's generosity and sociability that are important in the book, not his behaviour as a father.

Mr Palmer becomes a father during the course of *Sense and Sensibility*, being married to Lady Middleton's sister, a woman of little intelligence. He is a more interesting minor character and looks set to go the same way as Mr Bennet, but without the wit. He routinely ignores his wife. His behaviour in the company of others is idiosyncratic, tending to rudeness. He redeems himself a bit by behaving more considerately at his house in Cleveland, but Austen has Elinor Dashwood sum him up by referring to "his Epicurism, his selfishness, and his conceit" (*SS* III.6.299). As a father he is described as "fond of his child, though affecting to slight it" (*SS* III.6.298). This is not going to turn out well, but it is not germane to the plot.

The first father to be measured against Austen's standards is Mr Bennet, the worst of them.

Chapter 1
Mr Bennet: The Complete Delinquent

Mr Bennet is described in the opening pages of *Pride and Prejudice* as "so odd a mixture of quick parts, sarcastic humour, reserve and caprice" (*PP* I.1.5). This does not do him justice. He is the most delinquent father out of all the candidates and he has the least excuse. He is a man of extremes. He is the most intelligent and the most perceptive of all the fathers, and certainly the most witty, having some of the best lines in the novels. He is also the most indolent, neglectful and careless. He is not the most profligate father (there is strong competition for this title), but he is imprudent about money. Fortunately for his family, he is also the luckiest. His family mostly turn out fine, but this is in spite of his behaviour as a father rather than because of it.

His financial situation is comfortable for as long as he is alive. His income is £2,000 per annum (about £150,000 in 2012). This is plenty, even for the support of a wife and five daughters. Unfortunately, it is entailed, which means that, at his death, his nearest male relative will inherit his property and the income that goes with it. His heir is Mr Collins, who introduces himself to the Bennet family in Volume I. Mr Bennet's wife and daughters will inherit nothing. Mrs Bennet has £4,000 capital of her own (say, £300,000 today) which would yield an income of £150–£200 (£10,000–£14,000) and that is it. So on Mr Bennet's death, her standard of living will collapse. She will lose her home, carriage and servants. There would be no government provision of any kind. Mrs Bennet would be dependent on her brother to support them all, and, while he is a successful businessman, he has a wife and children of his own to care for. The outlook would be bleak.

Since his marriage, Mr Bennet has proceeded on the basis that he will have a son, and saving and economy would therefore be unnecessary. He has spent to the limit of his income (although not beyond it, which is why he is not top of the profligate league). He has no savings, no emergency pot of money. He has no plan B if it turns out he has no son. It was poor planning on his part to assume he would have a son in the first place. Childbirth was a hazardous business and infant mortality was high. When the novel opens it has been sixteen years since Lydia, the youngest daughter, was born; yet even in that period he has put nothing aside. The result is that his wife and daughters are dependent upon his survival for the provision of a roof over their heads and meals on the table. Another consequence is that when Wickham has to be paid, effectively, to marry Lydia following his elopement with her, Mr Bennet's brother-in-law, Mr Gardiner (as Mr Bennet thinks at the time) has to find the money to do it. When Mr Gardiner sends the terms for the settlement with Wickham, Mr Bennet doubts (rightly) whether he has seen the half of it: "Wickham's a fool, if he takes her with a farthing less than ten thousand pounds" (about £700,000 today), adding the typically cynical comment: "I should be sorry to think so ill of him, in the very beginning of our relationship"(*PP* III.7.305). He resolves to pay back Mr Gardiner by instalments. This is a humiliating position to be in, and he feels it, but this is the only point in the book where he shows any shame or remorse about his lack of spare funds.

The Bennet household is therefore precarious. Mr Bennet himself appears blithely oblivious to his family's reliance on his continued existence, apart from when he makes a joke of it. Heralding Mr Collins's first visit, he cheerfully tells his family: "when I am dead, [Mr Collins] may turn you all out of this house as soon as he pleases"(*PP* I.13.62). Mr Bennet may be only in his forties, but life was much more uncertain then than it is now (as the Dashwoods discover in *Sense and Sensibility*). When Mr Collins, Mr Bennet's heir, is to marry Charlotte Lucas, daughter of the Bennets' neighbours, Charlotte's mother looks forward to the day when Charlotte, as Mr Collins's wife, will take up residence at Longbourn instead of the Bennet family. She ruthlessly calculates how much longer Mr Bennet may live. Mrs Bennet is acutely aware of this and complains to Mr Bennet: "it is very hard to think that Charlotte Lucas should ever be mistress of this house, that *I* should be forced to make way for *her*, and live to see her take my place in it!" (*PP* I.23.131). Mr Bennet can only offer the consoling thought that she may not live to see it because he may outlive her. With Mr Bennet displaying this degree of insouciance about a very real risk, no wonder Mrs Bennet is going round the bend.

The various TV and film adaptations of *Pride and Prejudice* make little of this problem and show no sympathy with Mrs Bennet's railing against fate and against her husband. She is treated as a purely comic figure, ridiculed by Austen and found ridiculous by the reader for her nerves and her catty social competitiveness. She is described in Chapter 1 as "a woman of mean understanding, little information, and uncertain temper ... The business of her life was to get her daughters married; its solace was visiting and news" (*PP* I.1.5). This is harsh, because the fact is that Mrs Bennet has her eye completely on the ball as far as the family's financial cliff edge is concerned. Her near obsession with getting her daughters well married is the only practical response to the Olympian detachment of her husband. There is nothing else she can do as a mother and a woman to avoid the risk of eviction and destitution on his death. She cannot take up employment or enhance their financial position in any way. She is helpless and at the mercy of events.

Mrs Bennet's fury with Elizabeth for refusing Mr Collins's proposal is entirely understandable in this context. The reader finds the proposal hilarious, which it is, but from Mrs Bennet's point of view it would have solved, at a stroke, the conundrum of her life. If the heir is married to one of her own daughters, there will be no eviction, at least not without some alternative means of support being offered. She rails against Elizabeth:

> Aye, there she comes ... looking as unconcerned as may be, and caring no more for us than if we were at York, provided she can have her own way. – But I tell you what, Miss Lizzy, if you take it into your head to go on refusing every offer of marriage in this way, you will never get a husband at all – and I am sure I do not know who is to maintain you when your father is dead. (*PP* I.20.114)

No, and no one else knows it either, including Mr Bennet, and he does not care.

This being a comedy, the reader is not supposed to dwell on these sordid financial details, and so they are presented mostly through the pantomime-dame style of Mrs Bennet's tiresome and repetitive harangues. This should not, however, obscure the fact that Mr Bennet has neglected his family's financial security quite inexcusably. The situation is only rescued when two of his daughters marry so well above their financial station that provision for his wife and other daughters ceases to be a problem. The fact that Jane and Elizabeth do marry so well is, of course, in spite of his failures as a father. He does nothing to improve his daughters' prospects of marriage or to regulate the behaviour of his family. In fact, he does his best to ensure that no gentleman would dream of marrying into the Bennet family.

It is obvious that Mr Bennet has not chosen his wife well. The fathers in Austen's novels who choose well (Sir Walter Elliot in *Persuasion*, General Tilney in *Northanger Abbey* and Mr Woodhouse in *Emma*) lose their wives long before the novels open. Sir Thomas Bertram in *Mansfield Park* has an indolent and not very intelligent or engaged wife. The death of Mr Dashwood in *Sense and Sensibility* means that he is not around to curb his widow's emotional excesses. In Mr Bennet's case, he looked no further than "youth and beauty, and that appearance of good humour, which youth and beauty generally give" (*PP* II.19.238) in his selection of a partner. Mrs Bennet, who must be just over forty, is still a head-turner. Mr Bennet describes her as being "as handsome as any of [their daughters]" (*PP* I.1.4). He lived to repent his superficial judgement. Austen sums up the Bennet marriage at the end of Volume II, but she does not tell the reader much beyond what could have been gleaned from the previous pages. Mr Bennet feels no affection, respect, or esteem as far as his wife is concerned. He makes fun of her openly. He withdraws from the family as much as he can. He does not "seek comfort … in any of those pleasures which too often console the unfortunate for their folly or their vice" (*PP* II.19.238), that is, he does not take a mistress or resort to drink or gambling. He finds solace in country pursuits and, mainly, his books. He finds amusement in laughing at the folly of others, including his wife's. He does not intervene to curb his wife's behaviour in company or to rescue Kitty and Lydia from their mother's undiluted indulgence. Yet the evidence of the damage being done is there for all to see.

Elizabeth, strongly attached to her father and his favourite child, has always recognised that he behaves badly to her mother. However, she does not realise the half of it until she reads of Darcy's reaction to her family, in his letter to her after she has refused his proposal. The full extent of the damage, which extends to the family as a whole from her father's behaviour, is pitilessly made clear:

> But she had never felt so strongly as now, the disadvantages which must attend the children of so unsuitable a marriage, nor ever been so fully aware of the evils arising from so ill-judged a direction of [her father's] talents; talents which rightly used, might at least have preserved the respectability of his daughters, even if incapable of enlarging the mind of his wife. (*PP* II.19 238–9)

And this is before the elopement of Lydia and Wickham.

Saddled with an uncongenial wife, who is leading at least two of his daughters astray and shaming the rest, Mr Bennet retreats to his library, the equivalent of the modern-day shed at the bottom of the garden. It is no doubt where he is going when he is "fatigued with the raptures of his wife" (*PP* I.2.8), having confessed that he has indeed visited the newly arrived and eligible Mr Bingley. He is constantly evicting intruders from his library, whether it be Mr Collins or members of his own family. He sits there every day after tea and goes there expressly to be free from the "folly and conceit [to be found] in every other room in the house" (*PP* I.15.72). Nowadays, detached fathers might spend long days at the office or in business-related activities to avoid their homes and families. For Mr Bennet, a man of leisure, his bolthole is the library.

Considering how well read he is, and "regardless of time" (*PP* I.3.12) when reading, he has no concern for the education of his daughters, even of the two eldest, his favourites. Austen adopts her trick of using a minor and not very admirable character to make the point: in this case, Lady Catherine de Bourgh, Darcy's obnoxious aunt and the Collinses' neighbour and patron. Lady Catherine's comment is made during her cross-examination of Elizabeth while dining at Rosings during Elizabeth's visit to the Collinses at Hunsford. Lady Catherine remarks that she is very surprised the Bennet sisters cannot draw, that only two of them play and sing, and that they have had no formal education and no governess. This is all despite the fact that Mr Bennet's income could have supported a governess (interesting to note that she has a pretty good idea what his income is, courtesy, no doubt, of Mr Collins). She exclaims: "No governess! How was that possible? Five daughters brought up at home without a governess! – I never heard of such a thing. Your mother must have been quite a slave to your education." Ha ha. Even Elizabeth smiles at this one. Elizabeth defends her father by saying, "such of us as wished to learn, never wanted the means. We were always encouraged to read ... Those who chose to be idle, certainly might" (*PP* II.6.166–7). This is the problem. They might, and they were. Lady Catherine rams her point home with her usual subtlety: "I always say that nothing is to be done in education without steady and regular instruction, and nobody but a governess can give it" (*PP* II.6.167). Mr Bennet has imposed no discipline of any kind, so that the girls have been left to their own devices. Jane and Elizabeth have a bent towards self-improvement, but even they are way behind the field marked out by Bingley's two sisters. Much as Elizabeth dislikes the Bingley sisters, she has to acknowledge that when they exert themselves, they can be charming and entertaining: "Their powers of conversation were considerable. They could describe an entertainment with accuracy, relate an anecdote with humour, and laugh at their acquaintance with spirit" (*PP* I.11.54).

A lack of formal instruction has left the three younger sisters ignorant, although Mary, the middle daughter, tries hard, to little effect. Her father's only reaction to her efforts is to make fun of her. In Chapter 2 of Volume I, when he is about to reveal that he has visited Mr Bingley, Mr Bennet invites Mary to comment on the forms of introduction: "What say you, Mary? for you are a young lady of deep reflection I know, and read great books, and make extracts." When she fails to find something to say, he merely says, "While Mary is adjusting her ideas, ... let us return to Mr Bingley" (*PP* I.2.7). He taunts her hard work, finding amusement in baiting her when he should be making what effort he can to turn her capacity for concentration into something of value to her. In considering which of his daughters Mr Bingley might be persuaded to marry, Mr Bennet remarks, "They have none of them much to recommend them, … they are all silly and ignorant like other girls; but Lizzy has something more of quickness than her sisters" (*PP* I.1.5). Even Jane does not make the cut. Mr Bennet believes his two youngest daughters to be "two of the silliest girls in the country" (*PP* I.7.29) and "uncommonly foolish" (*PP* I.7.29). It is, of course, his fault that all this is largely true. Given that the Bennet girls need to marry to survive, Mr Bennet should have been compensating for their relative lack of fortune by educating them to the highest standards he could afford in order that they would stand out in the marriage market as attractive partners. He gives no thought to how the younger three are going to achieve this. Lydia pays heavily for his neglect.

Formal education is not the only thing lacking. Mr Bennet's failure to make them think at all about ethical principles and right behaviour leaves his daughters on the borders of respectability, and in Lydia's case, results in her overstepping them. They are not taught to distinguish between acceptable and unacceptable behaviour. Mr Bennet does not even show them by example how to behave, so absorbed is he in finding targets for his laconic sense of humour. When Elizabeth and Mr Gardiner are pondering whether Lydia could really have eloped with Wickham without being married to him, Elizabeth observes:

> But she is very young; she has never been taught to think on serious subjects; and for the last half year, nay for a twelvemonth, she has been given up to nothing but amusement and vanity. She has been allowed to dispose of her time in the most idle and frivolous manner, and to adopt any opinions that came in her way. (*PP* III.5.284)

Lydia's is the egregious case, but Kitty is nearly as bad, and Mary is fast becoming a female equivalent of Mr Collins in her tiresome and pompous pronouncements. Even Lizzie is censured by her mother, following one of her early impertinent exchanges with Darcy, by being told not to "run on in the wild manner that you are suffered to do at home" (*PP* I.9.42). Although valuing his two elder daughters, Mr Bennet does absolutely nothing to inform, guide or correct them or the other three. It is a case of "*sauve qui peut*". He deplores the behaviour of the youngest three, but takes no active steps to show them how to do better. As a result of his disengagement and his cavalier disregard of his family's predicament, Lydia's actions threaten to engulf the whole family in ignominy, while the family's lack of respectability robs Jane of Bingley, at least temporarily.

Darcy's letter of explanation to Elizabeth, following her refusal of his proposal and the accusations she makes against him, is in Chapter 12 of Volume II. It is a turning point and fittingly comes about half way through the novel. It marks the point at which a number of things come together: Darcy determines to mend his high-handed behaviour; Elizabeth begins to realise that he is The One; and her eyes and the reader's are opened to the infamy of Wickham, turning the tide of opinion in favour of Darcy. The letter also lays bare how an interested outsider sees the behaviour of the Bennet family: "The situation of your mother's family, though objectionable [i.e. they were in trade], was nothing in comparison of that total want of propriety so frequently, so almost uniformly betrayed by herself, by your three younger sisters, and occasionally even by your father" (*PP* II.12.200). Elizabeth makes herself face the truth of this and its consequences for Jane's attraction to

Bingley. She regards the faults of her family as "hopeless of remedy. Her father, contented with laughing at them, would never exert himself to restrain the wild giddiness of his youngest daughters; and her mother, with manners so far from right herself, was entirely insensible of the evil" (*PP* II.14.214–15). She returns from her visit to the Collinses' home at Hunsford mortified and depressed: "Jane's disappointment [over Bingley] had in fact been the work of her nearest relations, and [as Elizabeth] reflected how materially the credit of both [of them] must be hurt by such impropriety of conduct, she felt depressed beyond any thing she had ever known before" (*PP* II.13.211). The family is a social basket case.

On Elizabeth's return, her father is so pleased to see her that he comes out with: "I am glad you are come back, Lizzy" (*PP* II.16.224), a startling admission from the normally taciturn Mr Bennet. Elizabeth then finds that the prospect of Lydia, and perhaps also Kitty, following the regiment, including Wickham, from Meryton to Brighton is under active discussion. Her sense of the fairness of Darcy's letter is reinforced by listening to the entreaties being made by Lydia and Kitty. Fired up by Darcy's critique, she tackles her father head on in a vain attempt to get him to intervene and prevent Lydia and Kitty from following the regiment to Brighton. Here is an example, frequent in Austen's novels, of the heroine trying to compensate for the inadequacies of the father and, as usual, failing. She does not have the authority and influence to change his attitude and behaviour. He either changes himself or nothing is achieved.

In respect of the Brighton proposal, Elizabeth makes an impassioned argument for curtailing Lydia's propensity to mischief. "She represented to him all the improprieties of Lydia's general behaviour ... and the probability of her being yet more imprudent ... at Brighton, where the temptations must be greater than at home" (*PP* II.18.232–3). Receiving no response beyond "Lydia will never be easy till she has exposed herself in some public place or other, and we can never expect her to do it with so little expense or inconvenience to her family as under the present circumstances", Elizabeth ploughs on. Her description of the risk to Lydia is vigorous and colourful, directly implicating Kitty and indirectly the rest of her sisters:

> Our importance, our respectability in the world, must be affected by the wild volatility, the assurance and disdain of all restraint which mark Lydia's character. Excuse me – for I must speak plainly. If you, my dear father, will not take the trouble of checking her exuberant spirits, and of teaching her that her present pursuits are not to be the business of her life, she will soon be beyond the reach of amendment. Her character will be fixed, and she will, at sixteen, be the most determined flirt that ever made herself and her family ridiculous ... Vain, ignorant, idle and absolutely uncontrouled! Oh! my dear father, can you suppose it possible that they will not be censured and despised wherever they are known, and that their sisters will not be often involved in the disgrace? (*PP* II.18.232–3)

This is a very determined assault on her father's languid approach. Mr Bennet's replies are the stuff of disinterest and irresponsibility. He avoids confronting the issue, taking the line of least resistance. He refuses to believe that, in so far as any potential lovers have been put off, they must be "squeamish youths [if they] cannot bear to be connected with a little absurdity" (*PP* II.18.233). It is more than an absurdity, as Elizabeth is trying to convince him; it is a matter of respectability and reputation, or what you might call the family brand. He has taken them down-market by failing to intervene in order to establish and maintain certain standards of behaviour. Elizabeth's retort to Lady Catherine, that Darcy "is a gentleman; I am a gentleman's daughter; so far we are equal" (*PP* III.14.357), is nominally true, but quite beside the point. The Bennets have become an embarrassment to themselves and others. They have sunk in the social scale.

Mr Bennet refuses to acknowledge the validity of Elizabeth's concerns: "Do not make yourself uneasy, my love. Wherever you and Jane are known, you must be respected and valued; and you will not appear to less advantage for having a couple of – or I may say, three very silly sisters" (*PP* III.18.234). He turns out to be right in the end, but only because of the happy coincidence that Lydia runs off with the only man who could provoke Darcy's intervention. In allowing Lydia to go to Brighton with the Forsters, Mr Bennet depends on the Forsters' good sense and Lydia's lack of fortune to keep her out of real harm. He opts for a quiet life (as he wrongly assumes) by consenting to the visit. His detachment is leading directly to a catastrophe. He is at least gracious about it later when it all comes unstuck, admitting to Elizabeth that her advice had shown "some greatness of mind" (*PP* III.6.300).

Following Elizabeth's failure to persuade her father to keep Lydia at home, Mr Bennet recedes from the story. Meanwhile, the relationship between Elizabeth and Darcy develops promisingly during the visit to Derbyshire with Mr and Mrs Gardiner. Just as Elizabeth allows herself to recognise her strength of feeling for Darcy, catastrophe strikes from Brighton. As news of the elopement breaks, Mr Bennet's first reaction is reported by a letter from Jane. He is described as bearing it better than Mrs Bennet, which may not say much, but it is reported on the assumption that Lydia and Wickham have married. When doubt is cast on this assumption, the reaction is different. If Lydia is in a sexual relationship with a man who is not her husband, this is a sin, and vice, and completely disgraceful. Mr Bennet could have prevented it had he exerted himself. Instead, he persuaded himself that the outing to Brighton carried no real risk, and the family reels from the shock of it.

Jane reports that Mrs Bennet keeps to her bed; "as to my father, I never in my life saw him so affected" (*PP* III.4.276); he is in "excessive distress" (*PP* III.4.277). Later Jane explains that she had never seen anyone so shocked. "He could not speak a word for full ten minutes" (*PP* III.5.293). Darcy, who is on hand to witness the immediate aftermath once Elizabeth receives the news, is distracted. Elizabeth believes he is distancing himself from her: "everything *must* sink under such a proof of family weakness, such an assurance of the deepest disgrace ... Lydia – the humiliation, the misery, she was bringing on them all" (*PP* III.4.279). Elizabeth sees this as an "early example of what Lydia's infamy must produce" (*PP* III.4.280); "The mischief of neglect and mistaken indulgence towards such a girl ... Not Lydia only, but all were concerned in it" (*PP* III.4.281). It is the ultimate contaminant of a family's reputation. Lydia has been allowed to ruin herself and her family owing to the negligence of her father who failed to instil some principles, or, if he could not manage that, at least save her from herself by refusing to give in to her wishes. The "mischief of neglect and mistaken indulgence" (*PP* III.4.281) is his.

Mrs Bennet may be prostrate with the news, but the reader finds her still capable of speech: "Blaming every body but the person to whose ill judging indulgence the errors of her daughter must be principally owing" (*PP* III.5.288). Mr Collins, writing to Mr Bennet after the event, believes that "this licentiousness of behaviour in your daughter, has proceeded from a faulty degree of indulgence" (*PP* III.6.298). For once Mr Collins gets it right. "Indulgence" is a word to look out for in Austen's novels. It is a warning. Austen believes that indulgent mothers (and in *Emma*, an indulgent father) do damage to their children. The tendency to indulge is natural, but it needs to be contained and controlled by the father. Indulging your impulsive desires is bad for you and for society. Civilised society depends on self-control and self-denial. Those who give in are not admired by Austen even if no harm comes of it. In this case, Mrs Bennet has completely indulged Lydia, Mr Bennet has done nothing to stop her, and disaster has occurred.

When the elopement has taken place without the marriage, Elizabeth observes to Mr Gardiner that Wickham may expect to get away without having to marry a penniless girl: "Lydia has no brothers to step forward; and [Wickham] might imagine, from my father's behaviour, from his indolence and the little attention he has ever seemed to give to what was going forward in his family, that *he* would do as little, and think as little about it, as any father could do, in such a matter" (*PP* III.5.284). This is a shocking reflection on Mr Bennet's likely reaction, but it is not far from the truth. Mr Bennet, once over the initial shock, and before the Gardiners return from Derbyshire, does stir himself to go to London to try to find the errant couple. However, this is futile, as he has no idea where to look, and no talent for dealing with practical problems. While he is away, Mrs Bennet has fits of the vapours worrying that he will find Wickham, feel obliged to challenge him to a duel and get himself killed in the process. Happily for her, Mr Bennet is the last father who would think of exerting himself in this way.

Once the Gardiners are back, Mr Bennet is persuaded to come back to Longbourn and await developments. His demeanour is sorely tested by Lydia's elopement, but by the time he gets back from his fruitless trip to London "he had all the appearance of his usual philosophic composure. He said as little as he had ever been in the habit of saying; made no mention of the business that had taken him away, and it was some time before his daughters had courage to speak of it" (*PP* III.6.300). He then teases Kitty on the subject of her likely running away. Eventually, after he retreats to his library to await developments, no doubt reading another book, the whole matter is settled by Mr Gardiner, working secretly in cahoots with Darcy, with "so little inconvenience to himself … his chief wish at present, was to have as little trouble in the business as possible … he naturally returned to all his former indolence" (*PP* III.8.310). This is the Austen equivalent of putting your fingers in your ears and shouting "La La La" until the problem goes away. Darcy himself waited until Mr Bennet had returned home from London so that he could deal with Mr Gardiner alone. This does not surprise the reader.

Mr Bennet is rescued from the dire consequences of his neglect, both moral and financial, by the intervention of Darcy, the hero. Motivated by his passion for Elizabeth, and by a sense of having concealed from the world, for reasons of his own pride, the true nature of Wickham's character, he is able to use his inside knowledge to find the errant couple. He then taps into his great wealth (he has an income of at least £10,000 a year, about £700,000 today) to pay off Wickham and his creditors. In exchange, Wickham must pay the price of marriage to Lydia. Since the bulk of the financial settlement is Darcy's doing, Mr Bennet is off the hook, even of repayment.

Elizabeth recognises that Lydia must marry Wickham to salvage some respectability. She realises the irony in wishing her sister to be married to a man whom she knows to be wicked. Mr Collins and Lady Catherine are in a competition to rub the Bennet nose in the disgrace of it all. In his so-called letter of condolence, Mr Collins refers to the distress as "proceeding from a cause which no time can remove" (*PP* III.6.297) and that "for the consolation of yourself and Mrs Bennet, I am inclined to think that her own disposition must be naturally bad, or she could not be guilty of such an enormity, at so early an age" (*PP* III.6.298). He and Lady Catherine and Charlotte all believe that "this false step in one daughter, will be injurious to the fortunes of all the others, for who, as Lady Catherine herself condescendingly says, will connect themselves with such a family" (*PP* III.6.298). So they are marked out in Meryton as a most unfortunate family, at least until Jane gets engaged to Bingley, when they are "speedily pronounced to be the luckiest family in the world" (*PP* III.13.351). This piece of luck cuts no ice with Lady Catherine, who, in her ill-judged attempt to warn Elizabeth off becoming engaged to Darcy, refers to Lydia's "infamous elopement":

> I know it all; that the young man's marrying her, was a patched up business at the expence of your father and uncles. And is *such* a girl to be my nephew's sister? Is *her* husband, is the son of his late father's steward, to be his brother? Heaven and earth! – of what are you thinking? Are the shades of Pemberley to be thus polluted? (*PP* III.14.358)

Fortunately for Elizabeth, Lady Catherine's visit has given Darcy hope. Lady Catherine tells him about Elizabeth's refusal to promise not to marry him. He is encouraged to take another shot at it. Lucky is indeed the word.

Having considered Mr Bennet's financial imprudence, his neglect of his daughters' education, and his failure to instil good moral principles where they were lacking, the question now is whether Mr Bennet has any redeeming features. There are some positive aspects here, but they are mixed with a degree of disinterest, which fits with his indolence and general neglect. He values Jane and Elizabeth, and Elizabeth is his favourite. When Jane and Elizabeth return from Netherfield after Jane has recovered from her cold, "their father, though very laconic in his expressions of pleasure, was really glad to see them; he had felt their importance in the family circle. The evening conversation, when they were all assembled, had lost much of its animation, and almost all its sense, by the absence of Jane and Elizabeth" (*PP* I.12.60). This triggers no alarm bells for him. He refuses to recognise that he has a real problem on his hands as far as his other daughters are concerned. When Elizabeth sets off for a visit to the Collinses at Hunsford, "The only pain was in leaving her father, who would certainly miss her, and who, when it came to the point, so little liked her going, that he told her to write to him, and almost promised to answer her letter" (*PP* II.4.153). He and Elizabeth share strong powers of observation and a sharp accompanying wit. This is clear from their reaction to Mr Collins. Upon reading Mr Collins's letter of introduction, Elizabeth asks if he can be a sensible man. Mr Bennet's reply is typical: "No, my dear; I think not; I have great hopes of finding him quite the reverse. There is a mixture of servility and self-importance in his letter, which promises well. I am impatient to see him" (*PP* I.13.65). Jane is too good-tempered and tolerant to have such an edge and does not share in their less than charitable reflections. She is not her father's favourite; only in Elizabeth does he find a kindred spirit.

Elizabeth knows how much her father values her and is anxious that she should not disappoint his expectations. In one of the funniest lines in a very funny book, he sides with her against Mrs Bennet in her refusal of Mr Collins's proposal: "An unhappy alternative is before you, Elizabeth. From this day you must be a stranger to one of your parents. – Your mother will never see you again if you *not* marry Mr Collins, and I will never see you again if you *do*" (*PP* I.20.113). Mrs Gardiner uses Mr Bennet's expectations of her in warning Elizabeth against developing a relationship with the penniless Wickham at a time when he is a general favourite in Meryton. She invokes Elizabeth's feeling for her father: "You have sense, and we all expect you to use it. Your father would depend on *your* resolution and good conduct ... You must not disappoint your father" (*PP* II.3.146). Elizabeth makes a playful reply, but the point has been taken: "My father's opinion of me does me the greatest honor; and I should be miserable to forfeit it" (*PP* II.3.146). There is indeed a strong relationship between the two of them, but Elizabeth is not blind to her father's faults.

In his favour, Mr Bennet would not dream of sacrificing his daughters' happiness to material considerations. When Mr Collins makes his proposal to Elizabeth, Mr Bennet is not interested in the financial benefits of having a daughter married to his heir, even if it would secure a roof over the heads of his widow and other daughters after his death. And when Charlotte Lucas becomes engaged to Mr Collins, his only reflection is that he was "gratified ... to discover that Charlotte Lucas, whom he had been used to think tolerably sensible, was as foolish as his wife, and more foolish than his daughter!" (*PP* I.23.128). But his interest does not go very deep. It is doubtful whether he would have put up a struggle had one of the three youngest daughters agreed to marry Mr Collins. Indeed, he might have made some effort to see if Mary, as the most bookish of his daughters, was interested in Mr Collins for herself. He chides Elizabeth over Jane having been crossed in love when Bingley suddenly leaves Netherfield for London, but he shows no concern about whether Jane is actually upset, whether her heart has been so touched that she is really unhappy. He merely remarks: "a girl likes to be crossed in love a little now and then. It is something to think of, and gives her a sort of distinction among her companions" (*PP* II.1.139). But he is also genuinely happy for Jane when she and Bingley do eventually get engaged. He reacts to events, but he does not intervene to do his duty by his family.

With Lydia's marriage to Wickham accomplished, Darcy permits Bingley to return to Netherfield to pursue Jane, and comes with him to Longbourn to see if he might yet have some luck with Elizabeth. Bingley, invited to shoot with Mr Bennet, finds to his surprise that he is "much more agreeable than his companion expected. There was nothing of presumption or folly in Bingley, that could provoke his ridicule, or disgust him into silence; and he was more communicative, and less eccentric than the other had ever seen him" (*PP* III.13.347). So he can be normal if he chooses. This is in contrast with Mr Bennet's reception of Mr Collins, who "was as absurd as he had hoped, and he listened to him with the keenest enjoyment, maintaining at the same time the most resolute composure of countenance, and except in an occasional glance at Elizabeth, requiring no partner in his pleasure" (*PP* I.14.69). As he says to Elizabeth: "For what do we live, but to make sport for our neighbours, and laugh at them in our turn?" (*PP* III.15.365). Well, actually, no. That's not right. If you have five daughters, you might think that one of the things you lived for was to protect their interests and promote their happiness. Not in this case.

Darcy's application to Mr Bennet for consent to marry Elizabeth fares less well than Bingley's application to marry Jane. Mr Bennet has no idea of Elizabeth's change of heart. He still believes Darcy to be a tiresome snob, and he is ignorant of Darcy's role in the Wickham marriage. Elizabeth knows that Darcy's request for consent will not be refused, but her father "was going to be made unhappy, and that it should be through her means, that *she*, his favourite child, should be distressing him by her choice, should be filling him with fears and regrets in disposing of her, was a wretched reflection" (*PP* III.17.376). The exchange between them is very affecting. He thinks she is out of her senses to accept a man she heartily dislikes, however rich. She struggles to explain that Darcy is not what she originally thought him to be. Her father warns her about the dangers of someone with her spirit and temperament marrying a man she cannot love or respect. He fears she is marrying for money. Of course, he has actually already given his consent: "[Darcy] is the kind of man, indeed, to whom I should never dare refuse any thing, which he condescended to ask" (*PP* III.17.377). It is impossible to imagine Mr Bennet having the energy and determination even to postpone his consent until he has spoken to Elizabeth. He just goes with the flow.

Passive to the end, he does at least exert himself to ensure that Elizabeth knows what she is doing: "Your lively talents would place you in the greatest danger in an unequal marriage. You could scarcely escape discredit and misery. My child, let me not have the grief of seeing *you* unable to respect your partner in life. You know not what you are about" (*PP* III.17.377). Mr Bennet shows here that he is conscious of having made a very great mistake when he married. It is the only occasion on which he does this, and it is therefore very moving that he acknowledges it to try at last to protect his favourite daughter from making a similar error. Of course, it is misdirected, as Elizabeth is at no such risk. Mr Bennet manages to exert himself only when it does not matter. Elizabeth insists she loves Darcy and then reveals Darcy's role in the Wickham marriage. Mr Bennet immediately resumes his normal behaviour. His comment is quick and typical: "So much the better. It will save me a world of trouble and economy ... but these violent young lovers carry every thing their own way. I will offer to pay him tomorrow; he will rant and storm about his love for you, and there will be an end of the matter" (*PP* III.17.378). He makes an effort to know Darcy better, concluding: "Wickham, perhaps, is my favourite; but I think I shall like *your* husband quite as well as Jane's" (*PP* III.17.380).

Mr Bennet's luck knows no bounds: he spends all his money, risking destitution for his surviving family should he die; he takes no notice of Mrs Bennet's behaviour as a wife or as a mother; he neglects his daughters' education, moral welfare and happiness; his family's behaviour puts off respectable and wealthy suitors for his two elder daughters; and his refusal to intervene and take a stand against Lydia's wildness brings the whole family to the brink of irreversible disgrace. Only he has the power within the family to rectify any of this and he refuses to use it, becoming reclusive and cranky. Nevertheless, with one leap he is free, all thanks to Darcy. Darcy is so rich that he can support all the Bennets if necessary, and indirectly supports the Wickhams. Darcy loves and marries Elizabeth despite her family's social handicaps and despite the bitter pill of becoming Wickham's brother-in-law. He shows great stoicism in this self-sacrifice, an aspect of heroism which Austen greatly admires. He permits Bingley to love and marry Jane. It is Darcy who rescues the Bennet family from the ignominy of the elopement, all at his own exertion and cost. The remaining younger sisters will benefit from the Pemberley connection, improving under the Darcy influence rather than moping at home under Mr Bennet's chronic neglect. So although Mr Bennet has breached every paternal duty in the book, there is no lasting repercussion for him. All is resolved by Darcy. The Bennets are saved only because Lydia runs off with Wickham. Darcy would not have felt himself honour bound to chase after anyone else to patch up a marriage. The hero is not merely the heroine's love interest, but the means of resolving the problems caused by the father, whether financial or ethical. Mr Bennet's life continues as before, but with access to the bigger library at Pemberley. Lucky does not begin to describe it.

Chapter 2
Mr Woodhouse: the complete dependant

Mr Woodhouse has a blinkered approach to life. In addition to wearing blinkers, he is constantly staring at a mirror: all he can see is himself, his needs, his concerns. His younger daughter, Emma, has the job of ensuring that the blinkers stay on and that the mirror stays polished. Her father is to be protected as far as possible from any intrusion into his narrow life of selfishness and self-indulgence. Conscious of his reliance on Emma, Mr Woodhouse professes a great deal of regard for his younger daughter. Indeed, the problem is that he has too much of the wrong sort of regard, unmixed with any consideration, or even appreciation, of what is best for her. He provides no guidance, imposes no discipline or restraint, does not insist on any standards of behaviour or achievement. He regards Emma as faultless. She is the most important person in his life. Indeed, she is the only important person, being the one who is responsible, on a day-to-day basis, for attending to his needs, real or imagined. These are many and various, and they recur relentlessly: providing him with the right sort of food; humouring his obsessive anxiety about his health; offering him some rather narrow amusements; ensuring selected company from amongst their neighbours; respecting his dislike of going out; indulging his addiction to everything staying the same, down to the smallest detail of the furniture. Since Emma unfailingly meets his expectations of comfort, reassurance and amusement, it is not surprising that he has put her on a pedestal. She is stranded on that pedestal. It is the object of the novel to take her off it, not only bringing her to recognise the flaws in her judgement and treatment of others, flaws induced by her father's unqualified praise, but also releasing her from her isolation as her father's dedicated carer without rupturing her relationship with him. This is going to be tricky.

One thing that does not trouble this heroine is money. She is described at the outset as rich, although no specifics are given (unusually for Austen, who likes clarity around this important aspect of her characters' lives; figures are mostly absent in *Emma*). It is clear that the Woodhouse wealth derives from investments, not land, as their property is small. Mr Woodhouse never seems to think about it and certainly does not use it as an instrument of power. His elder daughter Isabella has married Mr Knightley's younger brother, John. As a younger brother, he has to work for a living. He is a lawyer. Mr Woodhouse cannot have had an issue with this. Money is not a weapon or an object for Mr Woodhouse. He does not use money as a stick or a carrot, as some other fathers in the novels do. He relies solely on emotional blackmail.

Mr Knightley, their unmarried next door neighbour and Emma's brother-in-law, is also rich, but he does have land. He is shown as a hands-on landowner, closeted with William

Larkins, his manager, and Robert Martin, his tenant farmer, explaining to his brother improvements being made to the estate. Frank Churchill, son to their neighbour Mr Weston, but brought up by his aunt and uncle, the Churchills, will be rich when they die. He is their heir, as they have no children of their own. Mr Weston is prosperous. Only Mrs Bates, her daughter Miss Bates (another woman looking after an elderly parent), and their niece Jane Fairfax are shown as poor, welcoming the gifts of food their neighbours bestow on them. Jane's lack of fortune is an issue in her engagement to Frank, despite his expectations. Mrs Churchill's attitude to Jane's lack of wealth and status is a problem, although it is possible that this selfish woman would object to any attachment Frank formed. So money looms relatively less large in this novel than in any of the others.

There is also no sexual misconduct, no elopements, and only Harriet Smith as the illegitimate child of somebody, who ensures from a distance that she is properly cared for. The greatest scandal is that Jane Fairfax and Frank Churchill are secretly engaged, which leads to all sorts of mischief. The only villain, if you regard Frank as being more romantic than unprincipled, is Mr Woodhouse himself.

Mr Woodhouse is not set up as any kind of ogre; it is rather the reverse. He is introduced clearly in Chapter 1 as "a most affectionate, indulgent father" (*E* I.1.3); that dangerous adjective "indulgent" is here unusually applied to a father, not a mother. He is formally courteous, taking trouble to welcome the Bates and Jane Fairfax when they come to dine: "The kind-hearted, polite old man might then sit down and feel that he had done his duty, and made every fair lady welcome and easy" (*E* II.16.288). His principal characteristics are: his "tenderness of heart ... which makes [him] so generally beloved" (*E* II.13.263); his extreme anxiety about his own health and well-being, and of others close to him; his fanatical resistance to change of any kind; and, last, but a long way from being least, his stupidity. This combination makes for a man of no imagination as to the thoughts, desires or feelings of others, who wishes to impose his own view of the world, and has absolutely zero tolerance of any activity that might upset his sensibilities. In short, he is supremely selfish, but so plainly without malice or any motive other than intending to do good, that he is generally liked and tolerated and, indeed, indulged, by all his relations and acquaintances.

In particular, he has inspired in his younger daughter, Emma, a degree of devotion rarely seen outside the cloister. She has dedicated herself to pandering to his every whim, protecting him from as much anxiety as possible, and entertaining him as best she can with the kind of dull society he welcomes. His wishes are attended to in meticulous detail. No demand is ever made of him. The vagaries of his disposition come first and are the stuff of much discussion and planning amongst his immediate circle. He is wholly dependent on Emma for his comfort and enjoyment. The net result is that he has locked Emma up at Hartfield quite as effectively as General Tilney locks up Eleanor in *Northanger Abbey* and with even less chance of release. These are serious charges against an apparently harmless old man and an invalid to boot. Can they be justified?

To begin with, he takes no interest in Emma's development or education. She is clever, but lacking in application. Mr Knightley is the one who points out Emma's failings in this respect. Recollecting that she drew up many worthy book lists, but never got around to reading any of the books, Mr Knightley observes: "I have done with expecting any course of steady reading from Emma. She will never submit to any thing requiring industry and patience, and a subjection of the fancy to the understanding" (*E* I.5.35); "Emma is spoiled by being the cleverest of her family. At ten years old, she had the misfortune of being able to answer questions which puzzled her sister at seventeen. She was always quick and assured" (*E* I.5.35). He laments the death of her mother, as "she lost the only person able to cope with her. She inherits her mother's talents, and must have been under subjection to her" (*E* I.5.35). Quite right, but then there would have been no story.

Mr Knightley is right, as ever, about Emma being a serial failure in her attempts to master a number of the usual accomplishments acquired by wealthy young ladies.

> She played and sang; – and drew in almost every style; but steadiness had always been wanting; and in nothing had she approached the degree of excellence which she would have been glad to command, and ought not to have failed of. She was not much deceived as to her own skill either as an artist or a musician, but she was not unwilling to have others deceived, or sorry to know her reputation for accomplishment often higher than it deserved. (*E* I.6.42–3)

She is ashamed to find that Jane Fairfax is a much better musician: "She did unfeignedly and unequivocally regret the inferiority of her own playing and singing. She did most heartily grieve over the idleness of her childhood – and sat down and practised vigorously an hour and a half" (*E* II.9.226). It is not very likely that there will have been any more hour-and-a-half-long practice sessions once she is no longer compared with Jane Fairfax. She has not developed the necessary powers of concentration and attention. Her drawing skills are also just short of what they could, or should, be: the likeness of Harriet, made for Mr Elton's benefit, shows Harriet as too tall. Mr Knightley irks her by pointing this out, although she does not admit to anyone but herself that he is right.

Her father's role in all this is merely to bestow praise, not to urge greater effort and concentration. The result of his disinterest is not as calamitous as Mr Bennet's laissez faire approach to education in *Pride and Prejudice*. In Mr Woodhouse's case, it derives from a lack of intelligent appreciation rather than from the studied disengagement which Mr Bennet turns into an art form. Mr Bennet has plenty of brains, which makes his faults all the more reprehensible. But Emma suffers, as the Bennet girls suffer, from a father's failure to insist on formal instruction and to expect some level of achievement. So she has an overblown sense of her abilities and shares with Elizabeth Bennet a good deal of misplaced conceit about her powers of judgement. Emma has no formal channel for her intelligence, and proceeds to wreak havoc with Harriet Smith's destiny before risking her own happiness with Frank Churchill and Mr Knightley. It is Mr Knightley who constantly tries to instil some caution and discretion, but Emma is obliged to discover her own errors before she at last submits to acknowledging how poorly she has judged others and herself. This painful process of self-discovery is the point of the book, but it stems from Mr Woodhouse's self-obsession and thoughtless praise of anything Emma does.

She has been left to her own devices for self-improvement and has made some progress because she is naturally clever. Her father thinks she excels, when she does not. Constant praise that is sometimes misplaced does not encourage diligence or a recognition that there is room for improvement.

There is a difference between encouragement to do better and thoughtless approval without constructive criticism. Mindless praise is recognised for what it is: evidence of not caring enough.

Mr Woodhouse was widowed while his two daughters were very young. He acquired a governess/companion to look after them in the form of Miss Taylor, to whom Emma owes such instruction as she has had. Miss Taylor proves to be another of Emma's uncritical fans: "the mildness of her temper had hardly allowed her to impose any restraint" (*E* I.1.3). She therefore compounded the problem, with the overall result that the "real evils indeed of Emma's situation were the power of having rather too much her own way, and a disposition to think a little too well of herself" (*E* I.1.3). "Evils" is a strong word to use in the context of a heroine who has beauty, brains, wealth and consequence, but Austen uses the word deliberately. Emma has much to unlearn.

Mr Woodhouse's own lack of brains presents another problem for Emma, especially in the wake of Miss Taylor's marriage to Mr Weston and her removal from the Woodhouse household. Emma genuinely loves, and is devoted to, her father. He cannot, however, respond to her or engage with her at her intellectual level: "She dearly loved her father, but he was no companion for her. He could not meet her in conversation, rational or playful" (*E* I.1.5). Her father cannot keep up with Emma in the most rudimentary of conversational sallies. When she points out that there is an inconsistency between his disapproval of marriage and his regret at not being able to visit the newly-wed Mrs Elton, he cannot understand that she is just teasing him a little, and he grows "nervous" (*E* II.14.274) as a result.

In the aftermath of the Weston/Taylor marriage, to which Mr Woodhouse will never be truly reconciled, Emma arranges a distraction for him by inviting Miss Bates, her mother Mrs Bates, and Mrs Goddard for the evening. Mr Woodhouse enjoys the company of Miss Bates because: "She was a great talker upon little matters, which exactly suited Mr Woodhouse, full of trivial communications and harmless gossip" (*E* I.3.19). At the end of the evening, Emma laments that this is a harbinger of many more such long and tedious (for her) evenings following the Weston/Taylor marriage: "the quiet prosings of three such women made her feel that every evening so spent, was indeed one of the long evenings she had fearfully anticipated" (*E* I.3 20). She is constantly engaged in the never-ending struggle to prevent her father from lapsing into melancholy. Following his customary nap after dinner, "her father awoke, and made it necessary to be cheerful. His spirits required support. He was a nervous man, easily depressed; fond of everybody that he was used to, and hating to part with them; hating change of every kind" (*E* I.1.5).

Mr Woodhouse's anxiety over his health dominates his view of the world. Austen is inexact about Mr Woodhouse's age, merely saying he "had not married early" (*E* I.1.5), but that may put him anywhere between fifty and seventy years old, that is, considerably older than his twenty-one-year-old younger daughter. Using the word "evil" again, Austen says:

> The evil of the actual disparity in their ages ... was much increased by his constitution and habits; for having been a valetudinarian all his life, without activity of mind or body, he was a much older man in ways than in years; and though everywhere beloved for the friendliness of his heart and his amiable temper, his talents could not have recommended him at any time. (*E* I.1.5)

Mr Woodhouse is quite conscious of the power he can exert as a result of his delicate health, saying to Mr Knightley: "We invalids think we are privileged people" (*E* I.8.55). When referring to his neglect of Mrs Elton as a new bride whom he should be visiting, he remarks that "it shews what a sad invalid I am!" (*E* II.14.273). He just revels in it.

His obsession with threats to his health causes him to interfere, if he can, with the harmless pleasures of others. In Chapter 1 he is troubled that the Westons even had, never mind distributed amongst their well-wishers, quantities of wedding cake, which he regards as unfit for human consumption. He tries to talk everyone out of eating any. He suggests that the wedding be put off when it rains a lot. Anything unfamiliar has to be unfolded very slowly and in small portions. When reading Mr Elton's riddles to him, Emma read "just as he liked to have any thing read, slowly and distinctly, and two or three times over, with explanations of every part as she proceeded" (*E* I.9.76). He is also a party pooper. The proposed outing to the Coles for dinner is a great occasion for displaying his selfish and blinkered approach. He declares himself "not fond of dinner-visiting … I never was. No more is Emma" (*E* II.7.205). This last remark is made without consulting her and is in fact quite wrong – she has a distinct inclination to go, but her wishes are presumed to be aligned with his. At last accepting that Emma will go, he turns to Mrs Weston to say "with a look of gentle reproach – 'Ah! Miss Taylor, if you had not married, you would have staid at home with me.'" (*E* II.7.205). Yes, indeed, the poor woman would have done exactly that and now it is not her problem; he may have intended to induce a guilt trip, but how she must have rejoiced in her new freedom. Then Mr Woodhouse's polite excuses to the Coles must be made by Emma on the basis of his being "quite an invalid" (*E* II.7.205). When Mr Weston suggests that Emma, given her social status in the neighbourhood, cannot politely leave the Coles' party early without the party breaking up, Mr Woodhouse remarks: "And no great harm if it does ... The sooner every party breaks up, the better" (*E* II.7.206). When the planned ball has to be put off, he is delighted: "it was shocking to have dear Emma disappointed; but they would all be safer at home" (*E* II.12.253).

Emma always has to have her father in mind when responding to any event, pleasant or unpleasant. When Harriet is importuned by the gypsies, Emma's first thought is to keep the information from him because it will make him anxious and alarmed, but this proves impossible as it becomes the talk of Highbury. The effect is as Emma predicted: "Poor Mr Woodhouse trembled as he sat, and, as Emma had foreseen, would scarcely be satisfied without their promising never to go beyond the shrubbery again" (*E* III.3.330). He has to be diverted from Knightley's decision to go "to London ... so suddenly ... on horseback, which she knew would be all very bad" (*E* III.9.380). He is affected by bad weather, during which "he could only be kept tolerably comfortable by almost ceaseless attention on his daughter's side" (*E* III.12.414).

Mr Woodhouse's resistance to change extends to the smallest things. Emma has talked him into replacing a small table with a large modern circular one, something only she could persuade him to do. His attitude to marriage as "the origin of change" (*E* I.1.5) is implacably negative. This is despite his own marriage, which suggests this was an attitude he slipped into in order to discourage others from disrupting his life. From his "habits of gentle selfishness" (*E* I.1.6) Mr Woodhouse is convinced that all others feel as he does, namely, that Miss Taylor herself would be happier staying with them than marrying Mr Weston. He finds it impossible to recognise that a woman who lodged with them as a companion to his younger daughter might jump at the chance of marriage to a prosperous and pleasant man in the neighbourhood, and of managing her very own household. Mr Knightley refers discreetly to Miss Taylor's "time of life" (*E* I.1.9), indicating that she was at, or just beyond, the normal age for marrying. He takes the economic view: "how important [it was] to her to be secure of a comfortable provision" (*E* I.1.9). Shades of Charlotte Lucas in *Pride and Prejudice*. Charlotte makes a brutal calculation based on her shortage of wealth and beauty and she sacrifices love for security; what a sacrifice it is for her. In Miss Taylor's case, there is no suggestion of romantic love for Mr Weston (he must be a good deal older than she is given that his son, Frank, is in his twenties), but there is affection and respect. Miss Taylor is sacrificing little when she abandons her post at Hartfield and throws in her lot with such a congenial companion. Miss Taylor may have made an even more calculating judgement: if Emma were to marry, then Miss Taylor's position would have been very difficult: either unwanted in the household of Emma and her husband, or wanted all too badly as sole remaining companion to Mr Woodhouse. Either way, she has escaped.

Mr Woodhouse's eldest daughter, Isabella, is another one who has got away. Her marriage to Mr Knightley's younger brother, John, continues to irk Mr Woodhouse: "he was by no means yet reconciled to his own daughter's marrying, nor could ever speak of her but with compassion" (*E* I.1.5). Indeed, he takes this to the point of resenting having to share Isabella with Mr Knightley on the first evening of the couple's visit, as he simply does not want to admit the claims of anyone else. In this case, Emma insists on Mr Knightley's right to dine with them, overruling her father. As with the replacement table, she is the one with authority in the household, but she will only insist against her father's wishes when it is really necessary.

Isabella is described as similar to her father in being something of a hypochondriac. When she arrives, she and Mr Woodhouse settle down for him to enjoy "a full flow of happy regrets and fearful affection with his daughter" (E I.12.98). Isabella is obsessed with her own health and that of her children. She loves talking to her father about maladies and remedies and would, from that point of view, have been a more natural companion for her father than Emma. However, having given birth to five seemingly healthy children, from whom Mr Woodhouse's nerves have to be protected, it is difficult to believe that her constitution is anything other than quite robust. This may be true also of her father. Those who fancy themselves delicate and who take precautions accordingly, often outlast others who are more carefree or careless. Emma cannot prevent Mr Woodhouse from grieving with Isabella over her journey, her trip to the sea and various medical issues. Despite Emma's best efforts, this eventually leads to a bad-tempered outburst from John Knightley who "had not always the patience that could have been wished. Mr Woodhouse's peculiarities and fidgettiness were sometimes provoking him to a rational remonstrance or sharp retort equally ill bestowed … [despite having] really a great regard for [him] and generally a strong sense of what was due to him"

(*E*.I.11.92). The reader can only wonder that he contained himself as well as he did.

One of John Knightley's roles in the book is to represent the reaction of a normal person to Mr Woodhouse's behaviour. The fact is that Mr Woodhouse requires gigantic amounts of attention, time, forbearance and patience, which a normal person would struggle to supply all day every day as Emma does. As we have seen, Mr John Knightley is occasionally provoked when he reaches the end of his tether with his father-in-law's fussing. This forces Emma to exert herself now and again, with occasional help from Mr Knightley, to turn the conversation. She is critical of her brother-in-law for his occasional outbursts, but the reader can only wonder how she copes. Mr Woodhouse's capacity to irritate knows no bounds, but most of those whom he encounters are at least tolerant of him. Importantly for the plot, this includes Mr Knightley.

Introduced in the first chapter as "sensible", Mr Knightley has "a cheerful manner which always did [Mr Woodhouse] good" (*E* I.1.7). "Sensible" is one of Austen's important labels, in the meaning of having a level of intelligence and using it. It amounts to high praise from Austen. Both Mr Knightley and his tenant farmer, Mr Martin, are described as sensible. Mr Allen, who takes Catherine Morland to Bath with his wife in *Northanger Abbey*, is described as sensible and intelligent. Captain Harville in *Persuasion* has a sensible countenance, as does Colonel Brandon in *Sense and Sensibility*. Nurse Rooke, also in *Persuasion*, is described as shrewd, intelligent and sensible. Charlotte Lucas in *Pride and Prejudice* is described as one of the very few sensible women who would have accepted Mr Collins. It is an adjective always worth looking out for in Austen's novels and not to be confused with sensibility, which is something quite different, as shown by her devoting an entire novel to the contrast.

Mr Knightley frequently walks from his own house to Hartfield next door, as he does in Chapter 1 when he returns from London and is introduced to the reader. He gently brushes aside Mr Woodhouse's needless fussing and moves on to other topics. When Mr Woodhouse is persuaded to accompany the strawberry pickers to Donwell Abbey, Mr Knightley goes to elaborate lengths to keep him comfortable and amused. "He wished to persuade Mr Woodhouse, as well as Emma, to join the party; and he knew that to have any of them sitting down out of doors to eat would inevitably make him ill" (*E* III.6.350). Mr Woodhouse takes a short walk in the driest part of the Donwell Abbey garden and then retires to sit in front of a fire (on a warm, sunny day in June), with various curios to look over and Mrs Weston for company. No child, invited to an adult occasion, would have had more effort expended on their amusement and comfort. Austen herself remarks on the resemblance, saying that he was "fortunate in having no other resemblance to a child, than in a total want of taste for what he saw, for he was slow, constant, and methodical" (*E* III.6.356). In this way, Mr Knightley marks himself out to the discerning reader (although it is unlikely that anyone gets it on first reading) as the only man capable of squaring Emma's marriage with the care of her father.

In discussing with Mrs Weston Emma's new project, Harriet Smith, Mr Knightley at once sees the dangers of raising Harriet's expectations above her station and realises that, as a naive and uneducated girl, she is no fit companion for Emma. He and Mrs Weston argue about it, Mrs Weston pointing out that Mr Woodhouse approves the acquaintance and only he can put a stop to it. Of course, there is unlikely to be an outbreak of paternal intervention from that quarter. As Mrs Weston says, Emma is "accountable to nobody but her father" (*E* I.5.38). The reader already knows that this is no accountability at all. Emma herself remarks to Harriet, "never, never could I expect to be so truly beloved and important; so always first and always right in any man's eyes as I am in my father's" (*E* I.10.83). This is true and that is the problem, although there is a catch – she is always first with her father only when he is always first with her. Constantly held up by her father as being in the right is something Mr Knightley sees as his duty to combat. He is the one who supplies the corrections and criticisms, which ought really to have come from her father. He is the only one who finds fault with her. It is Mr Knightley who provides the guidance and reproof that a father should offer, filling a very large vacuum as best he can, despite Emma's lack of appreciation for his trouble until she realises that she must marry him. In short, he is the only one who loves Emma enough to care about her behaviour. That is why she has to love him back.

Not only is Mr Woodhouse ineffectual in curbing or directing Emma, he also has reversed the usual roles of parent and child so that he constantly looks to Emma for all his daily needs. The intensity of her care for him is matched only by his dependence on it. She looks after him as if he can do nothing for himself, with the result that he *can* do nothing for himself. He looks to her to supply the kind of society and entertainment that he can tolerate and enjoy. In extreme conditions he expects her to supply solutions to problems. When there appears to be some risk of being stranded by the snow at Randalls, his reaction is to turn to her: "'What is to be done, my dear Emma? – what is to be done?' was Mr Woodhouse's first exclamation, and all that he could say for some time. To her he looked for comfort; and her assurances of safety" (*E* I.15.124). Once his anxiety has been excited, the only option is to take him home.

The overall picture, therefore, is of a daughter caught at home with her querulous, hypochondriac, irritating, endlessly demanding father, a father who has no conversation and who is absolutely no fun. He has no appreciation of the sacrifice that he expects, and which she makes. And this is only the beginning of Emma's problems. In these circumstances, she has no life of her own and her prospects of marriage are slim. Mr Knightley gets to the heart of the novel when he remarks to Mrs Weston: "There is an anxiety, a curiosity in what one feels for Emma. I wonder what will become of her!" (*E* I.5.38). Her antipathy to marriage is well known. She has said she will never marry. She tells Harriet, in a well-known outburst of authorial cynicism, that she has "none of the usual inducements to marry":

> Were I to fall in love, indeed, it would be a different thing! … without love, I am sure I should be a fool to change such a situation as mine. Fortune I do not want; employment I do not want; consequence I do not want: I believe few married women are half as much mistress of their husband's house, as I am of Hartfield. (*E* I.10.83)

Of course, she leaves out the companionship, the sex and the children, but she has a point if love is not involved. Mr Knightley takes this aversion to marriage with a pinch of salt, but acknowledges that there is no one in the vicinity likely to appeal to her, and she never goes anywhere else. He also acknowledges that love would make a difference to her: "I should like to see Emma in love, and in some doubt of a return; it would do her good" (*E* I.5.38–9). Mr Knightley always knows what is best for Emma, but he does not yet see that he might be able to fulfil that role for her, and the reader does not see it either.

In response, Mrs Weston, ever practical, points out the real problem: "I cannot wish her to be forming any attachment which would be creating such difficulties, on poor Mr Woodhouse's account" (*E* I.5.39). The vulgar and officious Mrs Elton gets straight to the point without caring whom she offends. Speaking of people's inclination or otherwise for visiting and exploring, she boldly remarks: "I perfectly understand your situation, however, Miss Woodhouse – (looking towards Mr Woodhouse) – Your father's state of health must be a great drawback" (*E* II.14.269). Recommending Bath, she adds:

> it could not fail of being of use to Mr Woodhouse's spirits, which, I understand, are sometimes much depressed. And as to its recommendations to *you*, I fancy I need not take much pains to dwell on them. The advantages of Bath to the young are pretty generally understood. It would be a charming introduction for you, who have lived so secluded a life; and I could immediately secure you some of the best society in the place. (*E* II.14.269)

Her presumption and vulgarity echo down the centuries, but Austen often makes her less admirable characters speak the truth, and Mrs Elton scores several direct hits in this short passage.

The premise is that Emma is not going to be in the way of meeting anyone she might marry unless she gets out of Highbury from time to time, and the demands made by her father rule out any visits to Bath or anywhere else. Indeed, she has not even seen the sea. She may represent the pinnacle of Highbury society – "The Woodhouses were first in consequence there" (*E* I.1.5) – but it is an isolated role. During the course of the book, which covers the period of a year, Mr Woodhouse ventures from home only twice: once to spend Christmas Eve with the Westons, which is remarked upon as an astonishing concession on his part, and once to Donwell Abbey to accompany the strawberry-picking party. It is so long since Emma has been to Donwell Abbey, which is next door to her own home at Hartfield, that she has to wander around and remind herself where everything is. With his resistance to change of any description and particularly to marriage, Mr Woodhouse has Emma effectively confined to Hartfield. It is not likely that she would let any suitor interfere with her duty to her father, and equally unlikely that any suitor would wish to take him on as part of a package.

Part of the plot is a supposed attachment between Frank Churchill and Emma, which Frank cultivates to distract attention from his actual attachment to Jane Fairfax. The Westons watch his apparent preference for Emma with complacency, as it is what they had hoped for by way of providing a suitable match for both the young people. Emma is conscious of the Westons' expectations. "Her own father's perfect exemption from any thought of the kind, the entire deficiency in him of all such sort of penetration or suspicion, was a most comfortable circumstance" (*E* II.5.188). Well, comfortable enough, unless and until some action has to be taken actually to marry. The Westons' plans for Frank to marry Emma stumble on the "difficulty of disposing of Mr Woodhouse ... How to settle the claims of Enscombe [the Churchills' estate in Yorkshire] and Hartfield had been a continual impediment" (*E* III.17.459). "Disposing" of Mr Woodhouse is certainly one way of looking at it. Unless disposed of by succumbing to death, there was no getting around the problem her father would have presented had Emma had to move to Yorkshire as a result of marrying Frank Churchill.

Emma's dutiful behaviour to her father is almost religious in its intensity. When Emma is mortified by Mr Knightley's reproof for her treatment of Miss Bates during the Box Hill outing, she spends the following evening playing backgammon with her father.

> *There*, indeed, lay real pleasure, for there she was giving up the sweetest hours of the twenty-four to his comfort; and feeling that, unmerited as might be the degree of his fond affection and confiding esteem, she could not, in her general conduct, be open to any severe reproach. As a daughter, she hoped she was not without a heart. (*E* III.8.371)

She is rude to Miss Bates, so she sacrifices her evening to her father to atone for her rudeness before going to make a conciliatory visit to Miss Bates.

Once Emma acknowledges the romantic nature of her own feelings for Mr Knightley, the issue of what to do about Mr Woodhouse reaches a crescendo. Her first thought is that she will be fine if Mr Knightley marries no one at all (she thinks at this point that Harriet is his object), so they could continue as before. She still thinks that marriage is not for her. "It would be incompatible with what she owed to her father, and with what she felt for him. Nothing should separate her from her father. She would not marry, even if she were asked by Mr Knightley" (*E* III.12.409). By this stage, Mrs Weston is pregnant and Emma recognises that the child will radically reduce the amount of socialising between the Westons and Hartfield, resulting in a denser concentration of time spent with her father. Frank Churchill will be at Enscombe and will take Jane Fairfax with him. The Eltons are outside the pale. The social whirl, which increases during the course of the book, suddenly starts to shrink again.

Against this background, Mr Knightley asks her to marry him and she finds herself able to accept. Finally, she takes a step away from her professed antipathy to marriage. She can no longer pretend to be hostile or indifferent now that she is in love. "Poor Mr Woodhouse little suspected what was plotting against him in the breast of that man [Mr Knightley] whom he was so cordially welcoming" (*E* III.14.426). Emma continues to be convinced that leaving her father is impossible: "a very short parley with her own heart produced the most solemn resolution of never quitting her father. – She even wept over the idea of it, as a sin of thought" (*E* III.14.427) (another religious reference). While he lived, they could only be engaged. So this apparently weak, frail, old invalid has a grip of iron over the destiny of his daughter, whose own happiness and fulfilment must give way to his selfish addiction to the status quo. She may not marry, enjoy companionship and sex, have children, or look forward to her own life independent of him. Mr Woodhouse is, in a different way, as selfish as General Tilney in *Northanger Abbey* – indeed, worse in this respect: even Tilney cheerfully lets his daughter go when the "right" man comes along.

Fortunately, Mr Knightley has been tackling the problem: "The impossibility of [Emma] quitting her father, Mr Knightley felt as strongly as herself" (*E* III.15.440). In a straight out fight with Mr Woodhouse over Emma, Mr Knightley knows he would lose. His first solution is to move Mr Woodhouse to Donwell with them. This is also his preferred solution, but he knows Mr Woodhouse well enough to realise that this is completely unrealistic. Such a move might risk his health, even his life. So he proposes to move in with them instead at Hartfield. Emma does not underestimate this offer: "he must be sacrificing a great deal of independence of hours and habits; that in living constantly with her father, and in no house of his own, there would be much, very much to be borne with." Too right. This is Mr Knightley being truly heroic, prepared to bear with stoicism and good humour the irritations of such a father-in-law.

Emma has to defer giving the news of her engagement to her father until Mrs Weston has had her child, since Mr Woodhouse cannot deal with too much anxiety at once. Finally, she puts it to him as positively as possible, but to no avail. His reaction is as negative as might be have been expected. "Poor man! – it was at first a considerable shock to him, and he tried earnestly to dissuade her from it" (*E* III.17.458). He reminds her of her resolution never to marry; in any event, he does not see that having Mr Knightley living with them is any improvement on what they enjoy of his company; she would be better off single, and so on. She toughs this out and enlists Mrs Weston's assistance in a gradual campaign to get him used to the idea. Mrs Weston is at first surprised, but quickly sees the advantages of making Hartfield the base. She recognises that no one "but Mr Knightley could know and bear with Mr Woodhouse, so as to make such an arrangement desirable!" (*E* III.17.459). In *Emma*, it is the hero who resolves the problem presented by the father, just as Darcy does in *Pride and Prejudice*. Emma can marry no one else.

So Mr Woodhouse is gradually softened up, but continues to regard the marriage as a "distant event" (*E* III.17.475). When first sounded out on the subject of a specific date, he is so miserable that they were almost hopeless. Emma nearly loses her nerve at this point: "She could not bear to see him suffering, to know him fancying himself neglected" (*E* III.19.475). The situation is retrieved, "not by any sudden illumination of Mr Woodhouse's mind, or any wonderful change of his nervous system" (*E* III.19.475), but by some local thievery, which makes Mr Woodhouse anxious for their personal safety at home. In this light, the addition of Mr Knightley to the household is suddenly attractive, and he agrees almost cheerfully to the marriage.

Right to the end, Mr Woodhouse thinks of nothing but his own concerns. This degree of selfish disregard for the feelings and well-being of his daughter borders on the cruel. Not once in the entire book does he make any remark that does not spring from his own interests and opinions. He would have stopped every marriage – from Isabella's to Miss Taylor's to Emma's – in the interests of keeping about him the people he depended on for his comfort and amusement. They are all women, of course.

Chapter 3
Mr Morland: a good father,
and General Tilney: the complete tyrant

Mr Morland, the heroine's father in *Northanger Abbey*, is a rare example of a good father. He has walk-on parts at the beginning and at the end. Early on in the novel he hands over his eldest daughter, Catherine, to his neighbours, who take her to Bath. Mr and Mrs Allen, the Morlands' wealthier and childless friends step into the parental role, chaperoning her in Bath until Catherine goes to Northanger Abbey. Mr Morland, his wife and family are the subject of quite extensive description in the first chapter of the book, and the manner of their despatch of Catherine to Bath takes up the second chapter. Apart from sending his consent to Catherine's acceptance of the invitation to Northanger Abbey at the end of Volume I, Mr Morland disappears totally from her life until she returns home, three chapters from the end. At that point, he makes an important decision regarding her engagement to Henry Tilney, showing his mettle as a father.

In the general spirit of ridiculing the Gothic novel, Mr Morland's prosperous and pedestrian circumstances are a matter for sarcastic comment at the beginning of the book where Austen describes Catherine's carefree and chaotic upbringing. She is the eldest of ten children and is expressly appointed the heroine of the book. Mr Morland's very ordinariness and sensible affection for his daughter are described by teasing the reader about the unrealistic extremes of character in the Gothic novel, where the heroine's father was usually the worst enemy of her welfare and happiness. Of course, this is also the case in Austen's own novels, but she makes the circumstances credible. Mr Morland is a clergyman, entirely respectable, comfortably off, with "a considerable independence, besides two good livings" (*NA* I.1.3). His precise financial status is important to subsequent events. He is not rich, but is sufficiently prosperous to bring up his ten children in some comfort. He teaches Catherine writing and accounts, two rather mundane skills not mentioned elsewhere in Austen's novels. Being "not in the least addicted to locking up daughters" (*NA* I.1.3), he stands in contrast to the principal father in the novel, General Tilney, father to Henry and Eleanor, who more or less does just that. When Catherine is invited to go to Bath with the Allens, Mr Morland consents willingly so that she can have some fun away from home. Consistent with being a good father, this quite significant trip is arranged in harmony with Mrs Morland: "Every thing indeed relative to this important journey was done, on the part of the Morlands, with a degree of moderation and composure" (*NA* I.1.9). Mr Morland's parting gesture is to pack her off with ten guineas for pocket money (£10 10s, or about £700 in today's money) and tells her to send for more if she needs it.

The Morlands do two more things from afar while Catherine is in Bath. The first is that they consent to her brother James becoming engaged to Isabella Thorpe. Isabella is anxious about whether they will consent, but Catherine has no doubts: "her father and mother would never oppose their son's wishes. – 'It is impossible … for parents to be more kind, or more desirous of their children's happiness; I have no doubt of their consenting immediately.'" (*NA* I.15.109). And they do indeed consent, but it does not go so smoothly for Catherine herself: some considerations are more important even than the happiness of children. The second thing they do is give consent for Catherine to go to Northanger Abbey. Then no more is heard of them until Catherine gets home. So Catherine sets off on her adventures to Bath and Northanger Abbey, trusting, naive, and not particularly clever, worldly-wise or well-informed, but ready to grow up and to cultivate her better judgement, especially of other people.

Austen describes Mr Allen, Catherine's temporary guardian, as sensible and intelligent, so he ranks high with the author, notwithstanding his choice of a monomaniacal fashionista as a wife. Mr Allen intervenes twice to look after the interests of his temporary ward. First, he checks out the Tilneys when Catherine has been introduced to Henry Tilney by the master of ceremonies in the Lower Rooms (speed dating, anyone?). He is told that Mr Tilney is a clergyman and that he comes "of a very respectable family in Gloucestershire" (*NA* I.3.20). He permits the relationship to develop. Later, he is rather tardy in his intervention to prevent John Thorpe from intervening in Catherine's friendship with the Tilneys. (Thorpe packs

Catherine off in his carriage to get her out of the Tilneys' way and into his own.) When Catherine returns early from one such outing, Mr Allen describes it as having been a "strange, wild scheme" (*NA* I.11.79). Eventually, he gives her his opinion that to drive about in open carriages to inns and public places is not right and he wonders that "Mrs Thorpe should allow it" (*NA* I.13.94). However, since Mrs Thorpe is in the "indulgent" category, the reader does not wonder at it at all. So Mr Allen provides Catherine with the determination she needs to resist further schemes of the kind and to focus on the Tilneys.

Here, Mr Allen is protecting Catherine without wishing to curtail proper enjoyment. But he insists on maintaining propriety and clearly regards outings in open carriages to public places as insufficiently supervised to be respectable. He is the one setting the rules and Catherine welcomes his intervention. It happens to sit with her own preference for getting rid of Thorpe's attentions, and she later comes to compare Mr Allen's attitude with that of General Tilney, who encourages her to sit with Henry in his curricle as they make their way to Northanger Abbey. Of course, this companion suits her better. The Allens drop out when Catherine goes to Northanger Abbey and make only a brief appearance at the end when Catherine has returned to her family.

Mr Morland resumes centre stage at the end of the book, taking a stand with respect to the engagement of Catherine and Henry. He cannot consent to their marriage, despite Henry's personal suitability and ample financial independence, unless and until the General gives his consent. Henry and Catherine may not take matters into their own hands. As usual with a good father, there is unity with the mother: "Their tempers were mild, but their principles were steady, and while his parent so expressly forbad the connexion, they could not allow themselves to encourage it" (*NA* II.16.233). The Morlands approve of Henry and recognise that their daughter has punched well above her weight when comparing her fortune to Henry's, but they will not budge while General Tilney maintains his formal objection. The fact that General Tilney is objecting for all the wrong reasons and has gone against basic decency in the way he dismissed Catherine from Northanger Abbey is neither here nor there. This exertion of authority against the preference and happiness of their daughter is clearly approved by Austen. She sees the principle of parental consent as trumping all emotional factors and she supports the Morlands' refusal as the right thing to do. The not-quite-yet happy couple have to bow before the exigencies of parental authority until a lucky break resolves the impasse. As far as Austen is concerned, this is exactly how it should be. A principled father acting in the interests of his daughter knows when to put his foot down, and he does it whether she likes it or not.

This degree of parental authority has evaporated today and does not always prevail in Austen's books. Parents, then and now, who object to friends, activities, or potential partners have only two levers to pull (assuming Gothic imprisonment is not available): money and disapproval. Whether either of these forms of intervention is effective is another matter altogether. So the Morlands had it relatively easy. Catherine was never going to defy their wishes and elope with Henry. Such subversive behaviour is not to be expected from the daughter of a good father.

Mr Morland's role in the plot is therefore threefold: he agrees to let Catherine go to Bath with the Allens, he is prosperous but not rich, making Catherine insufficiently attractive as a daughter-in-law for Tilney's greedy motives, and he makes a stand against any marriage to which all parents have not consented. He is most important as a standard bearer for the ordinary, affectionate and sensible father, married to an equally sensible woman, and bringing up his large family to know and observe good and respectable principles. In short, dull as ditchwater and not interesting material for a story.

So the first chapter of *Northanger Abbey* is spent making it clear that the heroine does not have the background or characteristics of the typical Gothic heroine: she is a very normal, not particularly sensitive or bright young woman, brought up in a happy, reasonably prosperous, stable and respectable family. Austen is flippant as she depicts behaviour and plot development which is the opposite of what one might expect in a Gothic melodrama, with one exception, namely Catherine's eviction from Northanger Abbey. As befits a novel that ridicules Gothic improbability, *Northanger Abbey* contains a gothically horrid father, albeit a realistic one. Austen plays a trick on her readers with the General. On the one hand, she tries to persuade her readers that the Gothic novel is just too preposterous to be taken seriously as literature, however entertaining it might be. On the other hand, she gives the reader a villain who is both Gothic and credible in order to show that it can be done. She does not need to resort to unrealistic events; she just shows the mundane mechanics of cruelty.

୶୶

General Tilney enters the novel quite late. Catherine has already met and taken a liking to his son, Henry, when his absence from the rooms in Bath is explained by his being out riding with his father. The following evening she is dancing with Henry when she sees that she is being stared at by a man who turns out to be General Tilney. "He was a very handsome man, of a commanding aspect, past the bloom, but not past the vigour of life" (*NA* I.10.70). She is impressed with his appearance and she follows his progress around the room with interest and admiration. So far so good. Following John Thorpe's successful ambushing of Catherine to prevent her keeping an engagement with the Tilneys, Catherine goes to the Tilneys' lodgings to apologise. She is refused entry, but sees them almost immediately leave the house. She thinks she has been snubbed owing to her own rudeness. Eleanor explains later that her father had been intending to walk out and "he being hurried for time, and not caring to have it put off, made a point of her being denied" (*NA* I.12.84). The discerning reader, but not Catherine, picks up a first clue that something is not quite right. The idea of being "hurried for time" when going for a walk while on a recreational visit to Bath is odd in itself. It was his doing that Catherine is refused entry to the Tilneys. This signals trouble.

Almost immediately after Eleanor gives this explanation at the theatre, Catherine spots John Thorpe talking to General Tilney, and talking, what is more, about her. Thorpe reports that the General is very rich and thinks Catherine "the finest girl in Bath" (*NA* I.12.86). Catherine and the reader take all this with a pinch of salt, coming from the boastful Thorpe, but subsequent developments show him to have been right on both counts, although the General has been deceived by Thorpe on the question of Catherine's wealth. The General admires Catherine because Thorpe has told him she is very rich. That the General was misinformed in this way is concealed from the reader until late in the book. After another of Thorpe's ambushes, Catherine finds herself at the Tilneys' lodgings at last, apologising again for breaking an engagement. As a result of the "solicitous politeness" (*NA* I.13.92) with which the General greets her, she recollects Thorpe's account of the General's admiration of her and thinks "[Thorpe] might be sometimes be depended on" (*NA* I.13.92). The General asks Catherine if "she would do his daughter the honour of dining and spending the rest of the day with her" (*NA* I.13.93). There is no sign that Isabella was consulted about this invitation being given; the General takes it upon himself to speak for her. Again, the discerning reader might smell a rat, but Catherine does not. General Tilney, however, cannot receive a visitor without finding fault with his servant. He is "quite angry" (*NA* I.13.92) that the door to the room was not opened for Catherine. As the General sees her out himself, he says "every thing gallant ... admiring the elasticity of her walk ... and making one of the most graceful bows she had ever beheld" (*NA* I.13.93). This is going too smoothly by half, especially in the excess of his compliments. Admiring the "elasticity" of someone's walk is just plain daft. Catherine has made her usual mistake of confusing what a person says with what they really are.

The first volume ends with Catherine determinedly misunderstanding Thorpe's proposal of marriage, made in the wake of Isabella becoming engaged to Catherine's brother, James. This provokes an exchange between Catherine and Thorpe that addresses a problem encountered by a number of characters in Austen's novels, namely, a disparity in wealth between two people who wish to marry. The problem affects Elizabeth and Darcy, and Jane and Bingley in *Pride and Prejudice*,

Frank and Jane in *Emma*, and Catherine herself and Henry Tilney in *Northanger Abbey*. Thorpe affects not to be interested in fortune because he has a good income. Whether or not this is true (coming from Thorpe, there has to be an element of doubt), it gives Austen the opportunity to deliver a homily on the subject through a pronouncement of Catherine's: "If there is a good fortune on one side, there can be no occasion for any on the other. No matter which has it, so that there is enough. I hate the idea of one great fortune looking out for another. And to marry for money I think the wickedest thing in existence" (*NA* I.15.114).

Austen shows characters of both sexes who are motivated by money when they marry. In *Pride and Prejudice*, Wickham stalks the rich Miss King, and will only marry Lydia if he is bought off; Charlotte Lucas has to snag Mr Collins to avoid becoming an old maid like Miss Bates in *Emma*. In *Sense and Sensibility*, Willoughby has to turn his back on Maria Dashwood and marry a woman for whom he has no regard because he needs her money. Lucy Steele finds that her engagement to Edward Ferrars can be broken if she can capture his better-off brother. In *Mansfield Park*, Maria Bertram wishes to escape from her parents' home to one of her own and to have a house in London. She likes to show off Mr Rushworth's great wealth (he is possibly even richer than Darcy). Also in *Mansfield Park*, Mary Crawford cannot bring herself to marry Edmund, whose means would be relatively modest and would not sustain a house in London. Gold-digging is alive and well in the novels.

Opposition to marriages where the fortunes are mismatched may come from the older generation not wanting a less wealthy or socially inferior connection (such as the Churchills' attitude to Mr Weston and, probably, Jane Fairfax, or Mrs Ferrars settling her wealth on Robert away from Edward when Edward's engagement to Lucy Steele becomes known). In the case of Bingley, it is his sisters and Darcy who voice their opposition to Jane Bennet. Sometimes there is a positive wish to unite fortunes (Lady Catherine's hopes for Darcy and her daughter; General Tilney's expectation of an addition to his family's fortune and status). On the other hand, Austen does not approve of marrying without the parties having the means to support themselves in respectability. The otherwise happy couple have to wait: Eleanor Dashwood and Edward Ferrars in *Sense and Sensibility*; Charles Hayter and Henrietta Musgrove in *Persuasion*. The Price family in Portsmouth show what life is like if you carry on regardless of your means (see Chapter 6 of this book).

By Volume II of *Northanger Abbey*, General Tilney has appeared little, but has been presented in a broadly favourable light as a handsome man, an admirer of Catherine and one who is encouraging her friendliness with Henry in particular. Early in Volume II, the tide begins to turn as Austen depicts Catherine's developing judgement of the General's behaviour. Keeping her appointment to dine with them (*NA* II.1.117), Catherine finds herself "most politely received" by the General, but neither Eleanor nor Henry behave like their normal selves: "[Henry] had never said so little, nor been so little agreeable; and in spite of their father's great civilities to her – in spite of his thanks, invitations, and compliments – it had been a release to get away from him". She is "puzzled" by this as he is "altogether a very charming man," being "tall and handsome, and Henry's father" (*NA* II.1.117).

Catherine's promising relationship with Henry seems set to fall by the wayside because General Tilney decides to leave

Bath early, owing to some friends he had expected not having turned up. Again it is his convenience that is consulted. All is well, however, because Catherine is invited to join them on a visit to their home. The invitation is given by General Tilney, "without leaving his daughter time to speak" (*NA* II.2.126). By this time Captain Tilney, the elder son, is in Bath, flirting with Isabella and receiving some encouragement despite her engagement to James Morland. Catherine assumes that the General will exert his authority over his son to take him out of the way of such behaviour, but Henry puts her right: no such action will even be considered. However, General Tilney makes his feelings known on the subject of the Captain being late for breakfast. Catherine is "quite pained by the severity of his father's reproof, which seemed disproportionate to the offence" (*NA* II.5.141). Captain Tilney bears this in silence, only whispering to Eleanor, "How glad I shall be when you are all off" (*NA* II.5.141).

The General's attitude to time-keeping, whether in relation to meals or other activities, was already hinted at when he refused to admit Catherine to their house because he was about to take a walk and had no time to spare for an unexpected visitor. This is a recurring theme in his behaviour: nothing puts him out of temper more quickly than being behind the schedule he has set for his day. His reaction to delays is indeed disproportionate and suggests some obsessive addiction to the timetabling of events that exerts a tyranny over those who are of his party and must fit in with his schedule. He has power and he likes wielding it. This is the negative side of parental, and particularly, paternal authority. If abused, it leads to misery, not happiness. Enjoying power, using it arbitrarily – even in trivial circumstances – capriciously changing objectives, demanding strict adherence to artificially imposed standards, never grateful, always critical, especially in front of others – this is a climate of fear.

The manner of the Tilney party's departure from Bath to travel to Northanger Abbey is another case in point. General Tilney is a nightmare travelling companion, making a bad-tempered and bossy palaver of getting them and the luggage into the coach. They are later in setting off than his appointed time of ten a.m., and various details of the travelling arrangements are wrong in ways that are not really important: "Had their party been perfectly agreeable, the delay would have been nothing; but General Tilney, though so charming a man, seemed always a check upon his children's spirits" (*NA* II.5.142). His "angry impatience" (*NA* II.5.142) at the inn lengthens Catherine's perception of the passage of time.

Once she is sitting more at ease with Henry in his curricle for the last part of the journey, Catherine hears how isolated Eleanor normally is at home. Henry describes her as "uncomfortably circumstanced – she had no female companion – and, in the frequent absence of her father, was sometimes without any companion at all" (*NA* II.5.143), Henry himself being often absent while he fulfilled his duties as a curate at his own house in Woodston. "Uncomfortably circumstanced" puts it mildly. The reader realises, as the book progresses, that Eleanor is, in effect, locked up by her father at Northanger Abbey. It is in a large property and not in a garret at the top of a tower, but she is confined nevertheless to a very lonely existence, and one from which she can only escape by marriage. And not just any marriage. It has to be one of which her father approves. Her father treats her as a companion and secretary. Late in the novel it turns out that he has prohibited her marriage to a man she loves because the hapless suitor is without status or fortune. Her only ticket out of Northanger Abbey is to find someone of status and fortune to marry. Given how little she gets out, her opportunities are not great. Even her visit to Bath, where she might find someone suitable, is curtailed by her father when it suits him to leave early.

It becomes apparent at Northanger Abbey that General Tilney really is very rich; Thorpe got that bit right. Catherine has to acknowledge that his property is more extensive than her family's and double that of the Allens. Catherine sees a "whole parish" (*NA* II.7.164) at work in the garden, and in the house she notices servants popping up everywhere. It appears that Henry is not dependent on his father financially; he has his own income from his curacy and will eventually be economically secure as a result of marriage settlements. When at last the way is clear for Henry to become engaged to Catherine, her parents acknowledge that, from a financial point of view, Catherine has hit the jackpot. The General does not, unfortunately, share Catherine's view, as she presented it to Thorpe, that one fortune is enough for two people. The General believes that one great fortune ought to be looking out for another.

While Catherine is falling for Henry in Bath, Thorpe puts a lot of effort into detaching Catherine from the Tilneys in order to get her for himself. Thorpe makes the mistake of boasting to General Tilney about the imagined extent of the Morlands' wealth and of Catherine's expectations from the richer Allens. Upon hearing this, and seeing that she has a preference for his younger son, General Tilney does everything he can to promote a match between her and Henry. When he takes Catherine to Northanger Abbey, he turns the tables on Thorpe by detaching Catherine from Thorpe's circle in order to capture her for Henry. General Tilney sees her as a prize asset. He is out to achieve exactly what Catherine thinks most wicked in marriage – to get his younger son to marry for money. The civilities in Bath, the invitation to Northanger Abbey, the trip to Henry's home in Woodston – the hints get heavier. He suggests that her family pay a visit, which Catherine feels as "an unexpected compliment, and deeply regretted the impossibility of thinking well of a man so kindly disposed towards herself" (*NA* II.8.171). This invitation and a reflection that he might perhaps soon have to buy another tea set, are hints that go over Catherine's head. By the time they visit Woodston, the allusions are so pointed as to be evident even to Catherine: he expects her to be living there as Henry's wife, the house needing only a woman's touch. He says explicitly that Henry could live comfortably on his living as a curate. Reflecting later on this visit, Catherine recollects that he "had so spoken and so looked as to give her the most positive conviction of his actually wishing their marriage" (*NA* II.14.215).

In fact, Catherine's family wealth is modest in comparison to that of the Tilneys. That this might become an issue first occurs to Catherine as a result of Isabella Thorpe's breach with James Morland and her succumbing to the charms of Captain Tilney. Catherine naively assumes that this will result in Isabella marrying the Captain, but his brother and sister doubt it. When Catherine tells them that Isabella's late father was a lawyer in Putney and that they are not a wealthy family, they doubt it even more. Catherine is surprised: "Your father is so very liberal! He told me the other day that he only valued money as it allowed him to promote the happiness of his children" (*NA*

II.10.190). This is indeed what he ought to feel, but Austen gives the reader a hint by describing the reaction of Henry and Eleanor thus: "The brother and sister looked at each other" (*NA* II.10 190). What the reader does not yet know, and does not learn until the end of the novel, is that General Tilney has already stood in the way of Eleanor marrying her own choice of husband owing to his being poor and without status. Catherine only knows that she is not much ahead of Isabella in the wealth stakes, but hopes that the General's evident partiality for her and his pronouncements on matters financial will result in her being acceptable. She hopes that his children have misjudged him.

General Tilney also has views on the employment of sons. The absence of work and consequent expansion of leisure time is one of the big differences between the life depicted in the novels and modern life. There are wealthy people who do not need to work today, but even the very rich usually occupy themselves, often very intensively, with their business interests or with charitable work. The General is an outlier in his attitude to work, given that it is quite unnecessary to the prosperity of either of his sons (there was no question of a daughter working – Eleanor has to put up with being kept at home until she marries). Referring to Henry's living, the General remarks to Catherine:

> Did Henry's income depend solely on this living, he would not be ill provided for … I am sure your father … would agree with me in thinking it expedient to give every young man some employment. The money is nothing, it is not an object, but employment is the thing. Even Frederick … who will perhaps inherit as considerable a landed property as any private man in the country, has his profession. (*NA* II.7.161–2)

Sir Thomas Bertram in *Mansfield Park* might usefully have taken a leaf out of this book in his management of his elder son, Tom, but it is of limited value in Captain Tilney's case. The Captain is shown as a philanderer (the reader wonders whether his dalliance with Isabella has extended to seduction) and somewhat disrespectful of his father. He must know that coming late to breakfast is a sure way of getting on the General's nerves, but he does it anyway. General Tilney likes to manipulate his children, but it is not always successful.

Apart from his greedy attitude to money and his willingness to use his children as bait to get more of it, General Tilney's generally selfish behaviour casts a pall all around him. Back on his home turf, his bad temper, and his expectation that everyone will conform to his norms of behaviour, show themselves in other situations. He spends so long showing Catherine around his extensive property, "proceeding to mention the costly gilding of one [apartment] in particular" (*NA* II.5.148), that he fails to notice there is little time to prepare for dinner. Catherine is late coming down. She and Eleanor find the General pacing the room, watch in hand. He pulled "the bell with violence, ordered 'Dinner to be on the table *directly*!'" (*NA* II.6.151). They are cheerful during the evening only when the General is absent. Feeling a bit washed out after a sleepless night of Gothic imaginings, Catherine has to suffer a "gentle hint of sympathetic early rising" (*NA* II.7.160). Under a veneer of pretending to find that Catherine would prefer to take a tour outside the house rather than in it, he is able to walk out at his usual time. When he at last leaves Catherine and Eleanor to their own devices, Catherine is "shocked to find how much her spirits were relieved by the separation" (*NA* II.7.165).

Later, when Eleanor has escaped the Tilney home by marrying, Austen refers to all the "hours of companionship, utility and patient endurance" (*NA* II.16.235) she had supplied to her father at home. He expresses concern at one point that Catherine might be becoming bored at Northanger Abbey, but presumably never considers his daughter's predicament. When Catherine is dismissed from his house, she reflects on what Eleanor "had been yesterday left to endure" (*NA* II.14.220). Following Henry's banishment for defying his father and refusing to break away from Catherine, Eleanor is left alone to "all the evils of such a home" (*NA* II.16.234). General Tilney spies on Eleanor's correspondence, as is evident when Eleanor asks Catherine to address letters "under cover to Alice" (*NA* II.13.213). General Tilney expects Eleanor to forego society, to think no more of the man she loves while he is poor and without rank. He would no doubt have found someone in due course who was rich and titled, and ordered her to marry him in much the same way that he orders Henry, first, to marry Catherine and, later, to give her up. Alternatively, he might have been quite happy to keep her at home as his companion and secretary rather than let her marry someone below his expectation. This is certainly how he makes use of her in the meantime.

Catherine continues to make the mistake of taking what the General says at face value. Advising Henry that he may expect a visit from them in Woodston, the General says there is no need to go to any trouble: "Whatever you may happen to have in the house will be enough. I think I can answer for the young ladies making allowance for a bachelor's table" (*NA* II.11.195). The consequence is that Henry leaves two days early, "Because no time is to be lost in frightening my old housekeeper out of her wits, – because I must go and prepare a dinner for you to be sure" (*NA* II.11.196). Catherine objects that "the General made such a point of your providing nothing extraordinary: – besides, if he had not said half so much as he did, he has always such an excellent dinner at home, that sitting down to a middling one for one day could not signify" (*NA* II.11.196). Not to a normal person, no. Henry knows his father better. Catherine found

> the inexplicability of the General's conduct dwelt much on her thoughts. That he was very particular in his eating, she had, by her own unassisted observation, already discovered; but why he should say one thing so positively, and mean another all the while, was most unaccountable! How were people, at that rate, to be understood? Who but Henry could have been aware of what his father was at? (*NA* II.11.196)

Catherine finds this very confusing, but Henry has his father's measure. When the meal is produced, Catherine

> could not but observe that the abundance of the dinner did not seem to create the smallest astonishment in the General; nay, that he was even looking at the side-table for cold meat which was not there. His son and daughter's observations were of a different kind. They had seldom seen him eat so heartily at any table but his own; and never before known him so little disconcerted by the melted butter's being oiled. (*NA* II.11.199)

No wonder Henry's housekeeper was likely to be frightened out of her wits at the prospect of the General coming to dinner.

When General Tilney has to go to London on business, the atmosphere at Northanger Abbey becomes immediately lighter and more relaxed. Catherine finds

> that a loss may be sometimes a gain. The happiness with which their time now passed, every employment

> voluntary, every laugh indulged, every meal a scene of ease and good-humour, walking where they liked and when they liked, their hours, pleasures and fatigues at their own command, made her thoroughly sensible of the restraint which the General's presence had imposed, and most thankfully feel their present release from it. (*NA* II.13.205)

Catherine has just agreed with Henry and Isabella that she will continue her stay with them beyond the four weeks she has already spent when the blow comes: Henry has to leave them briefly for Woodston. In that interval, the General unexpectedly returns late at night and delegates Eleanor to tell Catherine that she must leave the house at seven thirty the next morning and make her own way home.

It is a genuinely Gothic moment. At the time, it cannot be explained. Catherine wonders if she has caused offence. Isabella can only say that: "He certainly is greatly, very greatly discomposed; I have seldom seen him more so. His temper is not happy, and something has now occurred to ruffle it in an uncommon degree; some disappointment, some vexation, which just at this moment seems important; but which I can hardly suppose you to have any concern in, for how is it possible?" (*NA* II.13.210). Catherine feels all the hurt and indignity of it:

> Turned from the house, and in such a way! – Without any reason that could justify, any apology that could atone for the abruptness, the rudeness, nay, the insolence of it ... And all this by such a man as General Tilney, so polite, so well-bred, and heretofore so particularly fond of her! It was as incomprehensible as it was mortifying and grievous. (*NA* II.13.211)

The explanation is that General Tilney now believes, again on the strength of John Thorpe's information, that Catherine is penniless. His children had never understood their father's partiality for Catherine and realise, at last, that his "almost positive command to his son to do everything in his power to attach her" (*NA* II.15.230) derived from his mistake as to her wealth. But it is too late. His son's feelings have coincided with his father's wishes, and by the time the instruction is reversed, the son cannot reverse his emotions to comply. At last Henry makes an heroic stand for his love, and defies his father – no small step. It is a step which is open to him only because he is financially independent. Nevertheless, defying his father takes nerve. The General is "accustomed on every ordinary occasion to give the law in his family; prepared for no reluctance but of feeling, no opposing desire that should dare to clothe itself in words, could ill brook the opposition of his son" (*NA* II.15.232), and he takes this disobedience badly. Henry stands his ground and there is a rupture. When Henry had been contemplating the possibility that his brother might marry Isabella Thorpe, he remarked "I do not envy his situation, either as a lover or a son" (*NA* II.10.190). In one of Austen's frequent ironic twists, Henry now puts himself in exactly that position. As a result of General Tilney's error in relation to Catherine's wealth, and in his eyes therefore, her suitability, the General's unbridled temper leads him to act, as the Morlands put it later: "neither honourably nor feelingly – neither as a gentleman nor as a parent" (*NA* II.14.219). It is Henry who explains this when he comes to visit Catherine to ask her to marry him: "The General had had nothing to accuse her of, nothing to lay to her charge, but her being the involuntary, unconscious object of a deception which his pride could not pardon, and which a better pride would have been ashamed to own" (*NA* II.15.229). The Morlands, however, will not sanction Catherine's marriage to Henry without the approbation of Henry's father. The happy couple are stuck.

Relief is at hand once Eleanor is able to marry her long-standing admirer by virtue of a lucky death: he becomes a viscount and rich. General Tilney consents to her marriage to the man he had previously found to be unacceptable because of his lack of money. He has absolutely no interest in whether the match will promote Eleanor's happiness and well-being. He cares only that it will greatly enhance his own status to have a titled daughter (and no mere lowly title either), whose husband also happens to have a fortune. With Eleanor disposed of in a manner that pleases the General, and having his elder son still in play, the General is persuaded to give way over Henry and is consoled by Catherine having £3,000 after all (about £200,000 today) and the possibility of something more from the Allens. This turn of events puts a certain amount of pressure on Captain Tilney, as the elder son, to deliver a daughter-in-law who more than makes up for Henry's lacklustre choice. This is not likely to be a problem. His prospects of inheriting substantial wealth from his father, together with his personal attractions, should have them queuing up. He is a philanderer, and to have a trophy wife with a succession of mistresses would likely suit him perfectly well.

Catherine's own assessment of the General has been deteriorating as her judgement develops, and she shifts from taking everything said at face value to realising that people are not as they seem. When Henry clears his father from the suspicions Catherine had formed about his role in the death of his wife, Catherine is mortified by her mistake, but "she need not fear to acknowledge some actual specks in the character of [General Tilney], who, ... she did believe, upon serious consideration, to be not perfectly amiable" (*NA* II. 10.185). Well, that is one way of putting it. By the time she has been turned out of his house, however, she has moved on, and she believes that in harbouring these suspicions of him, "of either murdering or shutting up his wife, she had scarcely sinned against his character or magnified his cruelty" (*NA* II.15.232).

Cruel is a strong word, but it applies to General Tilney. Austen herself refers to the delay in Catherine and Henry's marriage as "occasioned by the General's cruelty" (*NA* II.16.236), and in her valedictory challenge to "parental tyranny" (*NA* II.16.236). She perhaps has her Gothic tongue firmly in her cheek here, but the fact is that General Tilney is cruel. There are two things he has got right: he has sufficient money to support his lifestyle, and he has educated his children to be discerning about books and art. But in all other ways, he is the antithesis of what a father should be. He is a martinet and regards his children as being under his absolute control. He bullies them, subordinates them to his whim, treats them like inanimate possessions, cares not for their happiness, expects absolute obedience from them, and will not vary his own habits to accommodate anyone else. For sheer nastiness, I think the prize goes to Mrs Norris in *Mansfield Park*, and Mr Elliot's claim, in *Persuasion*, to be the most ruthless and selfish schemer cannot be overlooked. But when it comes to Austen's community of fathers, General Tilney stands out as an actively unpleasant man with no redeeming features; his children could be so many prize cattle. Without his negative character traits, however, there would be no story. Had he adhered to the principle of valuing money only in so far as it could forward the happiness of his children, he would neither have been interested in Catherine's financial status in the first place, nor stood in the way of her marriage to Henry. Had he not been duped by Thorpe into believing that Catherine was rich, her relationship with Henry would not have been promoted by him; in particular, she would not have been invited to Northanger Abbey. Henry himself might not have been committed to Catherine but for his father's encouragement in the first place, and then by his father trying to wield power over him by ordering him to break off the relationship. To those who wonder why the clever and accomplished Henry should be committed to a naive girl like Catherine, they might just consider that there is nothing like a good dose of parental opposition to strengthen attachment.

Chapter 4
Sir Walter Elliot: The Witless Peacock

Persuasion begins with a description of one of Austen's most ridiculous, but nevertheless destructive fathers, Sir Walter Elliot: "Vanity was the beginning and the end of Sir Walter Elliot's character; vanity of person and of situation" (*P* I.1.4). He is fascinated by his own good looks, even at fifty-four, and by being a baronet from a line of some vintage and not one of the recent upstarts. "He considered the blessing of beauty as inferior only to the blessing of a baronetcy, and the Sir Walter Elliot, who united these gifts, was the constant object of his warmest respect and devotion" (*P* I.1.4). Clearly devoid of sense himself, he had lost his wife some thirteen years before the book opens. Like the late Mrs Woodhouse in *Emma*, Mrs Elliot might have been the saving of her daughters and, indeed, of her husband because she was "a wife of very superior character to any thing deserved by his own" (*P* I.1.4). But she unfortunately died, as she had to do for the purposes of Austen's story. At the time of his wife's death, Sir Walter had three quite young daughters: "an awful charge rather, to confide to the authority and guidance of a conceited, silly father" (*P* I.1.4). At the opening of the book, his youngest daughter, Mary, is married to Charles Musgrove junior, and his two eldest are unmarried; Elizabeth is twenty-nine and Anne is twenty-seven – no spring chickens these.

Since his wife died, a friend and neighbour, Lady Russell, has been a companion to Anne, but is not close to Elizabeth. There had been a general expectation that Sir Walter might marry Lady Russell, but he has not remarried, apparently not wishing to displace the claims of his existing daughters. Having no son, Sir Walter's title and estate will pass to a Mr Walter William Elliot, who is estranged from the family. Like Mr Bennet, Sir Walter cannot help the fact that he has no son to fulfil the entail, but he can ensure that his daughters will not be destitute at his death. One way to reduce that risk would be for one of his daughters to marry the heir, a similar situation to that of Mr Collins in *Pride and Prejudice*. In contrast to Mr Bennet, Sir Walter is all for it. He had planned a marriage between Elizabeth and Mr Elliot some years before. Mr Elliot had dallied with them a little, raising expectations, but he had elected, in the end, to marry elsewhere. His wife was of low social status but she was rich. She has since also died. Elizabeth had been disappointed, and now, although wearing well and still handsome, she feels (rightly) that age is stealing upon her. Her father may like to console himself by reading the details of his entry in the Baronetage, but it irks her to see her age coldly set out in print. Similar to her father in looks and attitude, Elizabeth is only interested in a man of rank and bearing, but these are not easily come by, especially if you have no fortune.

Sir Walter does not value Anne. She "had been a very pretty girl, but her bloom had vanished early; and as even in its height, her father had found little to admire in her, (so totally different were her delicate features and mild dark eyes from his own); there could be nothing in them now that she was faded and thin, to excite his esteem" (*P* I.1.6). Her looks are what count with him. She has lost them, so he has given up on her. He discounts Mary's marriage to the eldest son of a local family, who own land and who are wealthy, because they are not titled. He perceives Mary's husband's family as the ones to benefit from the connection with the Elliots. "Elizabeth would, one day or other, marry suitably" (*P* I.1.6). Or, then again, she may not. She is paying dearly in terms of her marriage prospects by holding herself at her father's estimation.

The importance of appearance is recognised by Austen, however much she may make fun of it with Sir Walter Elliot. She is not at all immune to the value of good looks in setting up her characters and their attraction to each other. In *Persuasion*, Sir Walter, his daughters, the Musgrove sisters, Captain Wentworth and Mr Elliot all have more than their fair share of good looks. Anne's beauty is rekindled under the influence of Captain Wentworth's presence. All the Tilneys are handsome in *Northanger Abbey* and Catherine Morland is also pretty. In *Pride and Prejudice*, Jane Bennet is beautiful and Elizabeth is "equally next to Jane in birth and beauty" (*PP* I.15.72). Darcy "soon drew the attention of the room by his fine, tall person, handsome features, noble mien" (*PP* I.3.10) – his housekeeper knows "none so handsome" (*PP* III.1.249). In *Sense and Sensibility*, Marianne Dashwood is beautiful and Willoughby's "manly beauty and more than common gracefulness were instantly the theme of general admiration"

(*SS* I.9.42) – clearly a complete knockout. Elinor plays second fiddle to Marianne in beauty, although very attractive herself. In *Mansfield Park*, Maria Bertram is beautiful, as is Mary Crawford, but Julia Bertram is another second fiddle. Fanny Price becomes beautiful as she grows into a young woman. Emma Woodhouse is beautiful and Mr Knightley, handsome himself, says that, "I have not a fault to find with her person … I love to look at her" (*E* I.5 37). Frank Churchill is handsome and Mr Knightley does not like him for it. Jane Fairfax is very elegant and Harriet Smith is pretty.

Most of Austen's heroines, however, are not vain. Fanny Price is oblivious of how pretty she has become. In *Emma*, Mr Knightley explicitly excuses Emma from personal vanity, although he thinks her not short of other faults. He acknowledges Jane Fairfax to be beautiful, but although she is not vain, "She has a fault. She has not the open temper which a man could wish for in a wife" (*E* II.15.282). In *Pride and Prejudice*, Elizabeth Bennet has her vanity piqued by Darcy initially finding her only "tolerable" (*PP* I.3.12), although by the time she has finished with him, he thinks her "one of the handsomest women of my acquaintance" (*PP* III.3.272). So good looks are an advantage, but both the possessor and the admirer of them must hold them at their proper value and not be distracted from the true worth of the person. Examples of those falling into the distraction trap are Mrs Dashwood with Willoughby in *Sense and Sensibility*, and Edmund with Mary Crawford in *Mansfield Park*. Sir Walter Elliot is all distraction.

It is no surprise that Elizabeth's aloofness and strong sense of dignity, copied from her father, have not made her many friends, even amongst her immediate family and acquaintances. When she and her father pay a family visit to Bath, their entrance "seemed to give a general chill. Anne felt an instant oppression, and, wherever she looked, saw symptoms of the same. The comfort, the freedom, the gaiety of the room was over, hushed into cold composure, determined silence, or insipid talk, to meet the heartless elegance of her father and sister. How mortifying to feel that it was so!" (*P* II.10.222). Mary has also picked up a share of her father's attitude to rank, which she shows in her assessment of Charles Hayter, the prospective husband of her sister-in-law Henrietta Musgrove. Her husband points out that she misjudges this because of Hayter's expectations, but she refuses to acknowledge, or is unable to grasp, the significance of a prospective inheritance.

Sir Walter's instinct to value everyone according to appearance and status, rather than for their intrinsic worth, may have led Elizabeth astray, but what drives the development of the story at the opening of the novel is not his vanity, but his profligacy. Unable to economise since his wife's death, he has been living beyond his means and has his head firmly in the sand on the subject. He has not been able to maintain a roof over their heads, despite it being perfectly possible to do so. He has the duty to provide for his daughters, but he has compromised his wealth and their expectations rather than make savings to add to his daughters' modest fortunes. Neither he nor Elizabeth can "devise any means of lessening their expenses without compromising their dignity" (*P* I.1.10). The estate is already mortgaged to the hilt. This sounds familiar. Overspending, indebtedness, juggling the payment of bills, defaulting on mortgage repayments, resistance to visible retrenchment which might compromise the family's standing in the community: the Sir Walters of this world are alive and well two hundred years on. Sir Walter eventually finds an acceptable path to balancing his books, but not before he has resisted some more obvious remedies.

A seven-year plan, designed by Anne and Lady Russell, is condemned outright as leaving him without "the decencies even of a private gentleman" (*P* I.1.13). His enjoyment of decencies that he can't afford leaves his unmarried daughters exposed to penury after his death. This is a serious breach of his duty as a father, but one to which he seems oblivious in the spotlight of his own self regard. So we have another Mr Bennet as far as finances are concerned; Sir Walter is older at fifty-four and therefore closer to death, heedless for the destiny of his unmarried daughters should he die. Mr Bennet in *Pride and Prejudice* did at least keep within his income, not out of financial prudence, but because his "love of independence had alone prevented their exceeding their income" (*PP* III.8.309). Sir Walter is too stupidly selfish to show any kind of restraint.

In trying to promote a plan of economy that will pay off the creditors and put the family finances back onto a sound footing, Anne Elliot tries to compensate for her father's weaknesses. As usual in Austen's novels, the attempt fails, but it has some effect. It provokes Sir Walter into saying he would sooner leave his home altogether than live there under shameful economies. Mr Shepherd, his lawyer and agent, pounces on precisely the solution he wished to promote: the letting of Kellynch Hall. This is the key event of the story, as it offers the opportunity to reintroduce Anne to her former fiancé.

Of course, "Sir Walter could not have borne the degradation of being known to design letting his house ... it was only on the supposition of his being spontaneously solicited by some most unexceptionable applicant, on his own terms, and as a great favor, that he would let it at all" (*P* I.2.15).

Mr Shepherd at last introduces the prospect of letting Kellynch to a naval officer returning to England, given that the hostilities with France are over. Sir Walter is rather against the navy for two reasons: "First, as being the means of bringing persons of obscure birth into undue distinction, and raising men to honours which their fathers and grandfathers never dreamt of; and secondly, as it cuts up a man's youth and vigour most horribly" (*P* I.3.19).

Eventually, Sir Walter is persuaded by the wily Mr Shepherd to let Kellynch to Admiral and Mrs Croft. When they meet, Sir Walter is pleasantly surprised to find "the Admiral to be the best-looking sailor he had ever met with" (*P* I.5.31). Mrs Croft has two brothers, one a curate, and the other a naval officer. The naval officer is Captain Wentworth, Anne's former fiancé of eight years previously. Their engagement had been disapproved of by both her father and Lady Russell:

> Sir Walter, on being applied to, without actually withholding his consent, or saying it should never be, gave it all the negative of great astonishment, great coldness, great silence, and a professed resolution of doing nothing for his daughter [i.e. no money]. He thought it a very degrading alliance; and Lady Russell, though with more tempered and pardonable pride, received it as a most unfortunate one. (*P* I.4.25)

So that was the end of that, and the beginning of Anne's decline from the pretty bloom of youth to being thin and haggard. In the meantime, having disapproved of Anne's choice and failed to bag his heir for Elizabeth, Sir Walter appears to have done nothing that might enable either Elizabeth or Anne to marry elsewhere. This is a cruel neglect, especially as he is eroding their fortune by his extravagant lifestyle.

Now Captain Wentworth, handsome, rich as a result of the war (worth £25,000, or over £1.5m in today's money), and still single, is coming in her way again. Anne has never met anyone to compare with him. She had previously turned down Charles Musgrove, who later married Mary instead. She holds out no hope of resuming the attachment to Captain Wentworth, given the brutal manner in which he was cast aside eight years earlier. She has been stoical about her fate for eight years and finds her resolve over the next few months sorely tested by events.

When Kellynch Hall is let, the plan is that the Elliots will move to Bath, where they can live more cheaply in rented rooms. One of the benefits of moving to Bath, as Anne and Lady Russell see it, is that Sir Walter will be taken out of the way of Mrs Clay, Mr Shepherd's daughter, who is now living with him again with her two children after a failed marriage (she is later described as a widow). She has caught Sir Walter's fancy and become a friend to Elizabeth. But when Sir Walter and Elizabeth decamp to lodgings in Bath, they leave Anne behind and take Mrs Clay instead. This indicates what a low opinion they both have of Anne. There is a risk that Sir Walter will marry Mrs Clay, which Anne clearly perceives. She tries to warn Elizabeth, but her fears are dismissed. The problem is not just that Mrs Clay is socially inferior and rather calculating in her behaviour. A remarriage by Sir Walter would compromise his daughters' position nearly as much as his death. Mrs Clay already has two children of her own and there is the possibility of more with Sir Walter. A new Lady Elliot would not feel obliged to accommodate either of the step-daughters. Anne consoles herself that, in this case, her security would lie in having a home with Lady Russell, but Elizabeth would have to marry to secure her future. This is therefore a source of real anxiety and a good example of contemporary sensitivity to the threat of destitution.

Anne is used to being slighted by her father and elder sister (this final Austen novel is unusual for showing two sisters who just cannot stand each other; the only other example is the relationship between Maria and Julia Bertram in *Mansfield Park*, who tend to sibling rivalry and fall out over Henry Crawford), and not a bit surprised to find Mrs Clay preferred to her. She also has a low opinion of her father; he has a low opinion of her; and, in turn, she has a low opinion of herself. It is all connected. Her attitude to her father is "a knowledge, which she often wished less, of her father's character" (*P* I.5.33) that leads her to recognise Mrs Clay as a real threat. Later, she is mortified by having to read Mr Elliot's opinion of her father thanks to her friend Mrs Smith, whose trust Mr Elliot has betrayed. Mrs Smith has a letter that Mr Elliot wrote following his earlier encounter with Sir Walter and Elizabeth when there was hope that he would marry Elizabeth:

> Give me joy: I have got rid of Sir Walter and Miss ... The baronet, nevertheless, is not unlikely to marry again; he is quite fool enough. If he does, however, they will leave me in peace, which may be a decent equivalent for the reversion [i.e. he will likely not inherit the title or the estate because Sir Walter may have a son]. He is worse than last year. (*P* II.9.200)

This grasping and calculating schemer does not mince his words, but they are to the point.

Since Anne is left behind when the others go to Bath, she is thrown in the way of Captain Wentworth, who comes to stay with his sister and brother-in-law at Kellynch. Also thrown in his way are Louisa and Henrietta, the two eldest of Charles Musgrove's sisters. Anne suffers agonies of misery and jealousy as he flirts with the pair of them and they with him. Eventually, following the accident at Lyme, Anne and Lady Russell join Sir Walter and Elizabeth in Bath. They find that Sir Walter and Elizabeth have ingratiated themselves with some distant cousins higher up the aristocratic pecking order: "Anne had never seen her father and sister before in contact with nobility, and she must acknowledge herself disappointed. She had hoped better things from their high ideas of their own situation in life, and was reduced to form a wish which she had never foreseen – a wish that they had more pride" (*P* II.4.146). Everywhere they go, they brag about the connection. It is demeaning.

The Crofts go to Bath, too, for the Admiral's gout. Sir Walter thinks they will be known there as his tenants. On their arrival Sir Walter "did, in fact, think and talk a great deal more about the Admiral, than the Admiral ever thought or talked about him" (*P* II.6.166). They are joined by Captain Wentworth. With Henrietta engaged at last to Charles Hayter, and Louisa, as a result of her accident, becoming engaged to Captain Benwick, the way is clear for Captain Wentworth's and Anne's reconciliation and re-engagement. Sir Walter and Elizabeth now begin to recognise that Captain Wentworth is a person of distinction. In giving him a card to a small party which Elizabeth is arranging, "The past was nothing. The present was that Captain Wentworth would move about well in her drawing room" (*P* II.10.223). Once he becomes reconciled with Anne, the wealth he now has as a result of successful naval campaigns (with the hope of more money if there are more wars) is essential because of Sir Walter's dire straits. If Anne is to be rescued from her father's poverty, she has to marry money.

Sir Walter's attitude to Anne's marriage is of a piece with his superficial and unintelligent approach:

> [He] made no objection ... [since Captain Wentworth] was now esteemed quite worthy to address the daughter of a foolish, spendthrift baronet, who had not had principle or sense enough to maintain himself in the situation in which Providence had placed him, and who could give his daughter at present but a small part of the share of ten thousand pounds which must be hers hereafter. (*P* II.12.245)

In other words, he has mortgaged her dowry, so she will have to wait for the rest of the £10,000 that should have been hers when she married. He does not rejoice in his daughter's happiness and good fortune:

> though he had no affection for Anne, and no vanity flattered, to make him really happy on the occasion, [he] was far from thinking it a bad match for her. On the contrary, when he saw more of Captain Wentworth, saw him repeatedly by daylight and eyed him well, he was very much struck by his personal claims, and felt that his superiority of appearance might be not unfairly balanced against her superiority of rank. (*P* II. 12.245)

What tosh, and what a lucky escape for Anne from her father's house.

Meanwhile, Elizabeth is disappointed a second time in her hopes of marrying Mr Elliot, her father's heir. He comes back on the scene as a result of hearing that his inheritance of the title is threatened by Mrs Clay's increasingly obvious association with Sir Walter. Suddenly, although already rich, courtesy of his first wife, he sees a title as icing on the cake and very much to be desired. His first idea is to marry Anne as a way of getting close to the family, and his attentions to her spark Wentworth's jealousy. She cannot be persuaded, and he eventually accepts that Anne will never be interested in him. His Plan B is to take off with the dangerous Mrs Clay. Of course, he does not intend to marry her, only to get her out of Sir Walter's way. So Elizabeth ends the story just as single and without prospects as when it began, and by that time she is thirty, not twenty-nine.

Anne is eventually rescued by her marriage to Captain Wentworth, but Elizabeth's prospects are bleak. Adopting her father's attitude to rank, she is fishing in a rather shallow pool. Her attitude to the possibility of marrying Mr Elliot shows her to be somewhat indifferent to true feelings. Her looks and status would not compensate for her lack of fortune in the eyes of many a potential husband. In short, by encouraging Elizabeth to proceed in life in accordance with his own shallow values and without a personal fortune, Sir Walter has put her at great risk. In the event of Sir Walter's death or remarriage, she would be dependent on one or other of her family, or on Lady Russell's charity. She is the ageing chatelaine of an indebted estate that must at last pass to the rogue Mr Elliot. She is the true victim of Sir Walter's inadequacies as a father to preserve his children from risk and penury.

֍

Persuasion contains two other fathers of interest: the elder Mr Musgrove and his eldest son Charles. The situation of the son has already been described in the Introduction. Charles Musgrove senior has a small but significant walk-on part in *Persuasion* as father to Charles Musgrove junior, and to Louisa and Henrietta. He is only one of two admirable fathers in Austen's novels, the other being Mr Morland in *Northanger Abbey*. We know that Austen thinks Musgrove and his wife are admirable because they are described, when they first appear in

Chapter 5 of Volume I, as being "in the old English style ... a very good sort of people; friendly and hospitable, not much educated, and not at all elegant" (*P* I.5.39). They are popular locally. Like the Morlands, they have a large family and, as with other successful parents, they are usually referred to as a couple, acting in unity. Their reaction to the events affecting their two elder daughters is the subject of comment from other characters, and likely reflects Austen's own opinion of how good parents should behave.

The first of these occurs when Louisa announces she is to marry Captain Benwick, rather than Captain Wentworth as had been anticipated. Captain Wentworth remarks that: "The Musgroves are behaving like themselves, most honourably and kindly, only anxious with true parental hearts to promote their daughter's comfort" (*P* II.8.180). Putting these words in the mouth of Captain Wentworth is a strong indication that this is what Austen thinks parents should aim for. When faced with both Louisa and Henrietta marrying more or less at the same time, the question of money arises. Mr Musgrove is well off but not rich, at least not in terms of ready cash (he does have property). His son remarks that his father might prefer the gentlemen to be richer, since he must provide portions to the daughters on their marriage and it will result in his having to make economies. But Charles adds that his father finds no other fault. Neither Mr Musgrove senior nor Charles begrudge this. Anne Elliot is prompted by this exchange with Charles to respond that Mr and Mrs Musgrove "seem so totally free from all those ambitious feelings which have led to much misconduct and misery" (*P* II.10.215). This is a telling remark in the context of the other novels where examples of such ambitious feelings abound (see, for example, Sir Thomas

Bertram's attitude to Maria's marriage to Rushworth in *Mansfield Park*). Mr Musgrove's behaviour as a father, being exemplary, does nothing to progress the story.

Chapter 5
Sir Thomas Bertram: a tragic figure

Sir Thomas Bertram, as the principal father and also a principal character in *Mansfield Park*, is a suitably subtle proposition. He assumes responsibility for Fanny Price, his wife's niece, when she is ten. His four children are older: Tom is seventeen, Edmund sixteen, Maria thirteen, and Julia twelve. Sir Thomas Bertram is a very different kettle of fish from his spendthrift and indigent brother-in-law, Mr Price (described in the next chapter), but he is unluckier in how most of his children turn out. His wife, Lady Bertram, is one of three sisters. She has the best of it in the wealth stakes. Her sister, Frances, marries Mr Price, a low-life naval officer. Miss Ward, the eldest, whose first name is never revealed, marries the Reverend Mr Norris. He is without fortune, but benefits from the largesse of Sir Thomas, who gives him a living.

Sir Thomas is benevolent and considerate. When Mrs Norris first proposes taking in Fanny, the eldest of Mrs Price's daughters, in order to alleviate the lot of the Price family, "He debated and hesitated; – it was a serious charge; – a girl so brought up must be adequately provided for, or there would be cruelty instead of kindness in taking her" (*MP* I.1.5). He has some concerns that one of his sons might think of marrying her. They are first cousins and permitted to marry. Such a connection would not be advantageous from his point of view. Having Fanny in the house from an early age might lead to such a relationship developing. Mrs Norris is sanguine. She believes that proximity is the best protection against such a risk: no mischief is likely to come of it when they are brought up as siblings. Sir Thomas is nevertheless concerned to "secure to the child, or consider ourselves engaged to secure to her hereafter, … the provision of a gentlewoman" (*MP* I.1.7). He "was fully resolved to be the real and consistent patron of the selected child" (*MP* I.1.8). He also takes care to assist the Prices with the education of their sons as they grow older. This is therefore a man who thinks carefully about the long-term implications of his actions, but he proves to be a poor judge in executing his decision and in anticipating how it will all turn out.

Despite Mrs Norris having no children of her own, she surprises Sir Thomas by refusing to take care of Fanny in her own home. Sir Thomas steps up and agrees to raise Fanny with his own children. "Yes, let her home be in this house. We will endeavour to do our duty by her, and she will at least have the advantage of companions of her own age, and of a regular instructress" (*MP* I.1.9). He has some concerns in case she turns out to have a very bad disposition. He expresses his low expectations of her state of knowledge and opinions, and the likely vulgarity of her manners. He believes he can cure her of these faults and he is right about that. He is also concerned to preserve the distinction of rank between his daughters and his niece, making it clear they are not equals, but ensuring that his daughters do not show too much arrogance. He regards it as a "point of great delicacy" (*MP* I.1.10) and looks to Mrs Norris to assist in maintaining the right balance. Lady Bertram is withdrawn and disengaged (the reader has to wonder if she is depressed). Mrs Norris is active and energetic. Sir Thomas is prepared to trust Mrs Norris to assume the day-to-day supervision of his two daughters and of Fanny. This turns out to be a great mistake on his part, which leads to all sorts of mischief for Maria in particular, and for Fanny. His faith in Mrs Norris is misplaced. Mrs Norris is a Cruella de Vil, and possibly the nastiest character in all Austen's novels, a cruel and spiteful bully, who is partial to and indulges Maria Bertram, rather neglects Julia, and delights in keeping Fanny in her place through a succession of nasty remarks and mean-minded actions. She resists and resents Fanny being favoured in any way. She is also mean as mustard and a first-class sponger. It is only after the theatricals have wreaked havoc that Sir Thomas begins to realise his misjudgement. He starts out believing that she was "one of those well-meaning people, who are always doing mistaken and very disagreeable things" (*MP* III.2.328), when she is not at all well-meaning, and most of her bad conduct is quite deliberate. She gets her just desserts in the end, but not before Sir Thomas has let her have too much rope by half.

Part of the problem is that Sir Thomas assumes that Mrs Norris will pass on to his children his values and principles because she is his wife's sister. Sir Thomas expects the busybody Mrs Norris to be actively teaching the three girls how to behave and to distinguish right from wrong. She is unsupervised and can let her personal preferences and resentments run riot. Outsourcing the girls' day-to-day care to Mrs Norris is all very well for practical purposes, but moral instruction needs to come from the parents. In this family, owing to Lady Bertram's indolence, it can only come from Sir Thomas, and he is not equipped to provide it effectively. Although well-intentioned, Sir Thomas has quite the wrong manner to endear himself to children, his own or anyone else's. This is a major handicap when it comes to teaching them how to behave in life. He has "a most untoward gravity of deportment" (*MP* I.2.12); his own daughters are in awe of him. When he takes Fanny in, he addresses them on the subject of Fanny with an "injudicious particularity" (*MP* I.2.12). Sir Thomas has no idea that anything is amiss: "though a truly anxious father, he was not outwardly affectionate, and the reserve of his manner repressed all the flow of their spirits before him" (*MP* I.2.19). Lady Bertram, although more affectionate, thought "more of her pug than her children, [but was] very indulgent [that word again] to the latter, when it did not put herself to inconvenience" (*MP* I.2.19).

The repressive effect that Sir Thomas has on his children and on Fanny is a weak echo of General Tilney's behaviour: it inspires fear, but neither affection nor respect. Like all the unsuccessful fathers in the novels, he is not at one with his wife, who cannot or will not supply the defect in his character of being unable to show the affection he feels, or to inspire the respect he deserves. Lady Bertram looks to Sir Thomas for a lead in all important things, and to her sister Mrs Norris for all unimportant ones. Austen shows that the Bertrams are not a well-suited pair when she describes Lady Bertram asking Sir Thomas to help her decide whether to play whist or speculation: he recommends the latter, because he prefers the former and "it would not much amuse him to have her for a partner" (*MP* II.7.235).

Sir Thomas himself has a very clear idea about what constitutes proper behaviour, but completely fails to communicate this to his children, Edmund apart. It quickly becomes clear that Edmund is the only principled child amongst the Bertrams. He is Fanny's favourite, her only protection from the callous behaviour of the family, and eventually the object of her love. The elder son, Tom, is profligate to the point of Sir Thomas having to make sacrifices himself, and on Edmund's behalf, to meet Tom's debts. In particular, when Mr Norris dies, the living has to be given to someone else rather than held for Edmund. This brings Dr and Mrs Grant into the neighbourhood (Dr Grant takes up the living). Sir Thomas's style of child management is shown in the appeal he makes to Tom's conscience when he has to dispose of the living in this way. He puts on "his most dignified manner" (*MP* I.3.23) in remonstrating with him: "You have robbed Edmund for ten, twenty, thirty years, perhaps for life, of more than half the income which ought to be his ... nothing can, in fact, be an equivalent for the certain advantage which he is now obliged to forego through the urgency of your debts" (*MP* I.3.23–4). Rather than feeling remorse for having "robbed" his brother, Tom thinks merely that "his father had made a most tiresome piece of work of it" (*MP* I.3.24).

In Chapter 3 of Volume 1, Sir Thomas has to leave for Antigua to attend to his business interests. He thinks it prudent to take Tom with him out of temptation's way. They are likely to be away a year, although Tom returns ahead of his father. Sir Thomas's daughters' reaction to his proposed departure does not augur well: "Their father was no object of love to them, he had never seemed the friend of their pleasures, and his absence was unhappily most welcome. They were relieved by it from all restraint ... they felt themselves ... to have every indulgence [here we go again] within their reach" (*MP* I.3.32). Even Fanny finds that she cannot be as sorry as she should. She later refers to how frightened of him she was when he checked her homework.

What happens in Sir Thomas's absence in Antigua over the next fifteen chapters is, of course, that the inhabitants of Mansfield Park, save for Fanny, go off the rails. At first Lady Bertram "was soon astonished to find how very well they did even without [Edmund's] father, how well Edmund could supply his place in carving, talking to the steward, writing to the attorney, settling with the servants" (*MP* I.4.34). As the remaining son at the property, it would be normal to look to him to assume the male role in the household. Then Maria meets Mr Rushworth at the local balls and, wishing at twenty-one for her own establishment and a house in London, she is inclined to make a match. This is actively promoted by Mrs Norris, who is delighted with Mr Rushworth's wealth and status (he has £12,000 a year; £800,000 today). She takes credit for promoting the relationship. Edmund is not convinced, concerned that Rushworth's income is his biggest, if not only, attraction. He is, however, helpless to influence the course of events in his father's absence. He finds it is easier to talk to the steward about the estate than to talk to his sister about her engagement. Sir Thomas's consent is supplied by post and the engagement is formed on the basis that the marriage will not take place until he returns. His return is regarded by the Bertram sisters as a "black" (*MP* I.11.106) moment, not to be looked forward to.

At this point the Grants at the parsonage introduce Mary and Henry Crawford, who are half sister and brother to Mrs Grant. They both have charm, looks, intelligence, sex appeal, perception and money. They are a very engaging pair. They prove to be a dangerously disruptive and, eventually, destructive influence. By this time, Tom has returned ahead of his father. Mary Crawford, just as keen on money as Maria Bertram, at first sets her cap at Tom as the elder son who will inherit the property. He is not interested and soon sets off for the racecourse and his friends. So Mary transfers her interest to Edmund, who is quickly caught by her attractions.

When the remaining party at Mansfield Park are invited for a day out to Rushworth's property at Sotherton Court, the Crawfords and Mrs Grant are invited too. This visit is a splendid, allegorical set piece. The ostensible reason for the visit is to consider some landscaping to the park. Henry Crawford is all for this and has lots of ideas about how nature can be improved. This fits with his power to disrupt and to destroy. When the visitors go outside to walk in the garden, woods and park, Fanny is left alone, feeling neglected and anxious, and giving occasional directions to those wandering in search of others. Edmund and Mary follow a winding path in the wood as she tries to lead him astray from his commitment to become a curate, a profession that does not suit her at all, either in its nature or its income. Maria, walking with Henry and Mr Rushworth, wishes to go through a locked gate to the park beyond. Mr Rushworth goes for the key, but Maria is impatient:

> '... unluckily that iron gate, that ha-ha, give me a feeling of restraint and hardship. I cannot get out, as the starling said.' As she spoke, and it was with expression, she walked to the gate; [Henry] followed her ...

> 'And for the world you would not get out without the key and without Mr Rushworth's authority and protection, or I think you might with little difficulty pass round the edge of the gate, here, with my assistance; I think it might be done, if you really wished to be more at large, and could allow yourself to think it not prohibited.'
>
> 'Prohibited! nonsense! I certainly can get out that way and I will. Mr Rushworth will be here in a moment you know – we shall not be out of sight.'

Henry and Maria then proceed around the gate and "By taking a circuitous, and as it appeared to [Fanny], very unreasonable direction to the knoll, they were soon beyond her eye" (*MP* I.10 98–9).

Maria is taking the initiative here, showing Henry that she does not care two hoots for Rushworth and is willing to be led astray in more ways than one. (She will later succumb to Henry's seductive charms and leave her husband.) Julia scampers after them round the gate, feeling left out and jealous of Henry's apparent preference for Maria. Rushworth, very peeved that they could not wait for the key, also goes in search of them. Everyone becomes out of sorts, but no permanent damage seems to be done. This is a false impression. Much mischief has had its origin in this outing. If Sir Thomas had been present, there would have been no random wandering about unsupervised, no defying locked gates, no unrestrained behaviour. The father's role is to ensure that the respectability of the family is not undermined by wandering from the conventional path into licentiousness.

The Bertram family, which Tom has re-joined, is bored at Mansfield Park. Without Sir Thomas to worry about, they find diversion in a theatrical project. Instigated by Tom's friend, John Yates, this venture causes all manner of damage – to personal relationships as well as to the fabric of the house.

Austen makes clear that Sir Thomas would not have found Yates's presence in the house at all "desirable" (*MP* I.13.120). Tom refers later to Yates having brought the theatrical "infection" (*MP* II.1.182) from another house. Thwarted in putting on a play elsewhere, Yates is determined. His suggestion is taken up with energy by all except Edmund and Fanny. Tom "was now master of the house" (*MP* I.13.122) and has assumed control at home in place of Edmund. Edmund tries to prevent any play-acting, but has no ally in his opposition to Tom, save for Fanny, who does not count for these purposes. His mother is happy to permit it. Mrs Norris sees an opportunity to shine and be useful. Edmund urges on Tom the impropriety of proceeding in the absence of their father abroad, where his safety is not certain, and also in light of Maria's engagement. This cuts no ice with Tom, who sees the absence of his father as an inducement and an opportunity, and as a means of distracting Lady Bertram from her husband's absence. They proceed to debate Sir Thomas's likely reaction. Edmund is convinced that he would "totally disapprove it" (*MP* I.13.125), but Tom appeals to his father's early encouragement of them play-acting at home in small parts. Edmund is unconvinced that he would be happy to see his adult daughters acting: "His sense of decorum is strict" (*MP* I.13.125).

Edmund is getting nowhere and falls back on urging that no formal stage should be made: "It would be taking liberties with my Father's house in his absence which could not be justified" (*MP* I.13.126). Failing to dissuade Tom, Edmund has to content himself with declining to act himself and then appealing to his sisters not to take part, with equally unsatisfactory results: "they were not in the least afraid of their

Father's disapprobation" (*MP* I.13.127). Edmund's attempt to take back from Tom a father's mantle of authority is a complete failure. All this argument occurs before the play is even selected. When it becomes apparent that the selection is *Lovers' Vows*, a romantic piece requiring all sorts of declarations of love, Edmund tries a further attack on Maria. This exchange causes Lady Bertram to exert herself so far as to say: "Do not act any thing improper, my dear ... Sir Thomas would not like it" (*MP* I.15.139). But Maria is not to be put off, conscious that Julia would pick up her part in a flash because of the opportunity it gave to act opposite Henry in romantic scenes. Lady Bertram has not the energy or interest to pursue the matter further; Mrs Norris supports Maria and Julia; and Edmund has to give up.

How is it that putting on a play at home is such a controversial proposition? The idea of going on the stage has long had rather disreputable associations as a form of licentious and unregulated behaviour. In this case, the question answers itself as the rehearsals proceed. The players are required to pretend to be characters and speak words that are not their own, and which represent feelings and desires that would be better suppressed. In particular, Maria Bertram and Henry Crawford act out scenes where they express their mutual attraction. Maria would clearly like the play to become reality. She is very strongly attracted to Henry and the play gives her every opportunity to express it under the thin guise of the play. The moral rot sets in and percolates through the company, except for Fanny. Yet even she has some doubts as to whether she is right to take a stand against taking a part (she is saved by Mrs Grant stepping in). Edmund betrays his principles by being inveigled into acting opposite Mary

Crawford and giving in to the very strong attraction he has towards her. He rationalises this because the alternative is to ask a neighbour to participate, but Fanny is not convinced. The rest of the troupe are delighted that Edmund has come off his high horse and joined in with the miscreants. Julia is driven to an excess of jealousy watching Maria and Henry. Rushworth is jealous of Crawford. Mrs Norris runs up curtains, managing to salvage some leftovers for her own use. The players flirt and squabble and bring in a carpenter to fit up a stage, physically altering the house. In short, they behave badly, dropping their emotional guard. It is a form of anarchy, with no regulation or oversight. Tom and the Crawfords are the principal instigators; Maria, Julia, Edmund and Fanny are the ones at risk.

In the course of the theatrical preparations, Mrs Grant and Mary Crawford discuss what Sir Thomas is to do on his return, beginning with putting Mr Rushworth up for parliament. Mrs Grant observes that Mary

> will find [Sir Thomas's] consequence very just and reasonable when you see him in his family ... I do not think we do so well without him. He has a fine dignified manner, which suits the head of such a house and keeps every body in their place. Lady Bertram seems more of a cypher now than when he is at home; and nobody else can keep Mrs Norris in order. (*MP* I.17.158–9)

This is all dead right. He is a dignified, respectable, head of the family, whose presence brings order. Unfortunately, he has some bits missing. Good judgement and an affectionate nature are left out. He inspires fear rather than respect and affection. These faults are to prove fatal to his expectations of how his children should behave.

Meanwhile, Mrs Norris is too busy making economies "for watching the behaviour, or guarding the happiness of his daughters" (*MP* I.17.160). She was never very good at either. Eventually, Fanny is once more under pressure from the company to take up a part because Mrs Grant has to leave to attend to her husband's indisposition,. On this occasion, Edmund joins the pack in bullying her to agree, and Fanny does not know how to resist further. She has just given in when "the door of the room was thrown open, and Julia appearing at it, with a face all aghast, exclaimed, 'My father is come! He is in the hall at this moment.'" (*MP* I.18.169). So ends Volume I. Everyone, except Fanny, knows that they have behaved indecorously and in a manner that has been morally degenerate. Now there is to be a reckoning.

The reaction to Sir Thomas's return is very amusing. The opening chapter of Volume II gets it perfectly: "consternation … absolute horror … unwelcome, most ill-timed, most appalling! … every other heart was sinking under some degree of self-condemnation or undefined alarm" (*MP* II.1.173). Fanny nearly faints as "all her former habitual dread of her uncle was returning" (*MP* II.1.174). The man himself is so happy to be home that he is more than usually unbending, informal and talkative: "the delight of his sensations in being again in his own house, in the centre of his family after such a separation made him communicative and chatty in a very unusual degree" (*MP* II.1.176). If only he had always behaved like this, his children might have respected him more and sought to meet his expectations of them. Sir Thomas greets Fanny with real affection and emotion. When she finally has "courage to lift her eyes to his face, she saw that he was grown thinner and had the burnt, fagged, worn look of fatigue and a hot climate, every tender feeling was increased, and she was miserable in considering how much unsuspected vexation was probably ready to burst on him" (*MP* II.1.176).

His delight is indeed to prove only temporary. He has already discovered the physical changes to the house and been confronted by Mr Yates rehearsing on his own before Tom arrives to make an introduction. Sir Thomas knows all about Tom's "friends", and on his return to the family group he already shows an "increase in gravity" (*MP* II.1.181). It can only be downhill from here for the thespians. Yates rattles on, unaware that Sir Thomas is glaring at him: "seeing Sir Thomas's dark brow contract as he looked with inquiring earnestness at his daughters and Edmund, dwelling particularly on the latter, and speaking a language, a remonstrance, a reproof, which *he* felt at his heart" (*MP* II.1.182). Sir Thomas does not pursue it on the spot, only referring to his dislike of "noisy pleasures" (*MP* II.1.184), but he has come home to find that his children and their friends have trashed his house under the noses of his wife and sister-in-law.

The following morning he has it out with Edmund, who excuses only Fanny from criticism. His father's reaction is exactly what Edmund predicted:

> Sir Thomas saw all the impropriety of such a scheme among such a party, and at such a time, as strongly as his son had ever supposed he must; he felt it too much indeed for many words; and having shaken hands with Edmund, meant to try to lose the disagreeable impression, and forget how much he had been forgotten himself as soon as he could. (*MP* II.2 185)

He then speaks to Mrs Norris of his disappointment that she failed to spot the impropriety and put a stop to it. He assumes, of course, that she would have had the authority to stop it in his absence, in opposition to Tom's wishes, an assumption which is not necessarily justified. Her only reaction is to change the subject. He still does not have her measure: "foiled by her evasions, disarmed by her flattery" (*MP* II.2.188). So Sir Thomas burns every copy of the play he comes across and dismantles the set.

Mr Yates is confounded and gives a very fair description of Sir Thomas's inability to inspire respect: "He had known many disagreeable fathers before, and often been struck with the inconveniences they occasioned, but never in the whole course of his life, had he seen one of that class, so unintelligibly moral, so infamously tyrannical as Sir Thomas" (*MP* II.2.189). The phrase "unintelligibly moral" is very telling. Yates recognises that Sir Thomas is trying to do what he believes to be the right thing, but he has absolutely no idea why Sir Thomas thinks it is the right thing. It appears arbitrary and without value except as a capricious exercise of power. Sir Thomas has completely failed to communicate to the young people what is wrong with their behaviour. Yates nevertheless sticks around for Julia's sake (a hint of what is to come).

The impact on the atmosphere is palpable. "Under [Sir Thomas's] government, Mansfield was an altered place" (*MP* II.3.193). The party is more sombre, less merry, although this is, in fact, a return to what it had been like before, rather than a new situation, as Fanny points out: "As well as I can recollect it was always much the same. There was never much laughing in [Sir Thomas's] presence ... I cannot recollect that our evenings formerly were ever merry, except when my uncle was in town. No young people's are, I suppose, when those they look up to are at home" (*MP* II.3.194). Well, not all parents are such killjoys and it is sad that this has been Fanny's only experience, but this is a house of extremes: when Sir Thomas is at home, no one has any fun; and when he is away, they all have far too much. The idea of spending "quality time" with his family would have been completely alien to him. He would have had no idea that it could have any purpose or value. Sir Thomas is so put out by what has happened in his absence that, while he is prepared to see the Rushworths, no one else, not even the Grants/Crawfords, are welcome at the house.

The evidence of the rehearsals may have been destroyed by Sir Thomas, but their effects linger. He may be able to eradicate the physical manifestations of the play, but he has no idea of the moral disintegration that has occurred. Maria's relationship with Rushworth has been undermined. She and her sister are unseemly rivals for Henry's attentions. As with Elizabeth and Anne in *Persuasion*, Maria and Julia are not sisterly soul mates. Edmund's feelings for Mary Crawford have made him betray the principles he had been so eloquent in propounding at the outset. Fanny is appalled at what she has witnessed, but not distracted by it. Maria is so passionate about Henry Crawford that she expects him to make a declaration to her. But he goes to join his uncle in Bath.

In this frustrated frame of mind, Maria is ill-prepared to deal with her father's misgivings about her engagement to Rushworth.

> He had expected a very different son-in-law; and beginning to feel grave on Maria's account, tried to understand *her* feelings. Little observation there was necessary to tell him that indifference was the most favourable state they could be in. Her behaviour to Mr Rushworth was careless and cold. She could not, did not like him. Sir Thomas resolved to speak seriously to her. Advantageous as would be the alliance, and long-standing and public as was the engagement, her happiness must not be sacrificed to it. (*MP* II.3.197)

When he tackles her, Maria is quite composed and confirms she is happy with her choice. Of course, she is not, but she is too resentful at Henry's desertion to say so. "Sir Thomas was satisfied; too glad to be satisfied perhaps to urge the matter quite so far as his judgment might have dictated to others. It was an alliance which he could not have relinquished without pain" (*MP* II.3.197–8). He takes her statement at face value. He consoles himself that she will be near the support of her family. He was "happy to secure a marriage which would bring him such an addition of respectability and influence, and very happy to think any thing of his daughter's disposition that was most favourable for the purpose" (*MP* II.3.198).

Sir Thomas borders here on the General Tilney approach to marital alliances that consequence and fortune are more attractive than they should be. As he realises later, this is a ghastly mistake. This puts him one up on General Tilney, who never has any self-doubt because in his case, events fall out in accordance with his prescription. Sir Thomas's failure to make a more determined intervention, which he knew in his heart he should do as Maria's father, leads to a marriage that cannot resist the wrong sort of temptation. Maria was not physically attracted to Rushworth: Austen makes it clear that he was not a sexually attractive proposition. Henry Crawford, on the other hand, confident and exuding sex appeal, probably an experienced lover, was just delicious. Maria developed a burning desire for him and was frustrated in more ways than one when he just turned around and set off for Bath. Henry knew that he could bide his time. Maria had shown, by passing around the locked gate at Sotherton, that she was prepared to be seduced. Henry, not wishing to marry her and not lacking other options, could afford to be cool about it.

Meanwhile, another favourable marriage may be looming. Sir Thomas very kindly insists, against Mrs Norris's recommendation, that Fanny should take the carriage to have dinner at the Grants rather than walk, which is what Mrs Norris thinks is appropriate. "'Walk!' repeated Sir Thomas in a tone of most unanswerable dignity" (*MP* II.5.218), an exclamation not unlike Lady Bracknell's "A handbag!" It is on this occasion that Henry Crawford, now returned to the Grants and bored with his easy conquest of the Bertram sisters, decides to take a tilt at Fanny's heart, at first for the fun of it, just because he can. By the time the Bertrams themselves go to dinner at the Grants, Sir Thomas thinks that Henry Crawford might admire Fanny. This is the beginning of a campaign waged against Fanny to persuade her to marry Henry Crawford. The campaign is much more serious than the pressure she came under to act in the ill-fated play because the assault is led by Sir Thomas himself. So, having made the mistake of not insisting that Maria consider her engagement to Rushworth more carefully, he proceeds to make the opposite mistake with Fanny by insisting that she gives serious consideration to marrying Henry Crawford. The man means well, but just has not got a clue.

Matters advance significantly at the ball at which Fanny "comes out", taking her place formally in society. Sir Thomas admires the outcome of his investment in her upbringing: "education and manners she owed to him" (*MP* II.10.272). This is true and it is an achievement. As the ball draws to a close, Fanny is exhausted and Sir Thomas "advises" her to take to her bed ("'Advise' was his word, but it was the advice of absolute power" (*MP* II.10.276)) and off to bed she goes. "In thus sending her away, Sir Thomas perhaps might not be thinking merely of her health. It might occur to him, that Mr Crawford had been sitting by her long enough, or he might mean to recommend her as a wife by shewing her persuadableness" (*MP* II.10.277). Sir Thomas has made a misjudgement, as he is wont to do, in this case about Fanny's steely resolve. She has endured much at Mansfield Park: contempt from the Bertram daughters, cruelty from Mrs Norris, jealousy and misery from watching Edmund, her only friend, fall for the superficial charms of Mary Crawford. This girl is another Austen stoic. She needs to be. Her trials are by no means over. Henry Crawford observes that Sir Thomas is kind to Fanny in his way: "but it is the way of a rich, superior, longworded, arbitrary uncle" (*MP* II.12.292). Here is another astute remark. He doubts what either Sir Thomas or Edmund can do for Fanny's essential happiness compared to what he might do. Crawford is, in fact, incapable of curbing his licentious habits and providing happiness to Fanny, but that is his tragedy. He is right about everything else.

Volume II ends with Fanny refusing to marry Henry, despite his role in advancing her brother William's career in the navy through the influence of his uncle, Admiral Crawford. Volume III opens with Sir Thomas making a very determined attempt to get Fanny to change her mind. It is objectively a very attractive match for her and one well above any reasonable aspirations she might have. The mere sound of Sir Thomas's distinctive step approaching Fanny's sitting room causes her to tremble: "a heavy step, an unusual step in that part of the house; it was her uncle's; she knew it as well as his voice; she had trembled at it as often, and began to tremble again, at the idea of his coming up to speak to her, whatever might be the subject" (*MP* III.1.308). Sir Thomas is blithely unaware of the effect he has: he is as emotionally sensitive as a robot.

The scene which follows is distressing. Sir Thomas has no idea why Fanny is so set against Henry Crawford, and she cannot explain herself without revealing Maria's and Julia's misconduct during the theatricals. She can only say that she does not like him well enough to marry him. Sir Thomas urges on her Henry's "situation in life, fortune, and character, but with more than common agreeableness, with address and conversation pleasing to every body" (*MP* III.1.311). Fanny "had hoped that to a man like her uncle, so discerning, so honourable, so good, the simple acknowledgement of settled *dislike* on her side, would have been sufficient. To her infinite grief she found it was not" (*MP* III.1.313). When he is finally convinced that she does really mean to refuse Henry, he speaks to her "with a good deal of cold sternness" (*MP* III.1.314) and delivers a long and wounding lecture on her lack of gratitude, the benefits to her family which she is abjuring, her stubborn nature, her selfish determination, and her folly in declining such an eligible match:

> … you have now shewn me that you can be wilful and perverse, that you can and will decide for yourself, without any consideration or deference for those who have surely some right to guide you – without even asking their advice … in a wild fit of folly, throwing away from you such an opportunity of being settled in life, eligibly, honourably, nobly settled, as will, probably, never occur to you again … Gladly would I have bestowed either of my own daughters on him … You do not owe me the duty of a child. But Fanny, if your heart can acquit you of *ingratitude* –. (*MP* III.1.314–15)

He reduces her to misery. This is Sir Thomas at his least appealing and most Tilney-like. He has no idea that Fanny might be the better judge of Henry Crawford. He uses every ounce of his paternal authority to bully her into marriage without considering that her feelings should be given due weight. He considers only the material advantages of the proposal for the security of Fanny's future, not her essential happiness. In this way, he shows why he is a failure as a father.

Having reported the refusal to Crawford, Sir Thomas does relent a little, although he still believes that Fanny might be persuaded in time to change her mind. He also remembers to change Mrs Norris's mean instruction that Fanny should never have a fire in her sitting room: he orders one to be lit there in future. These small acts of kindness show a side of him that he would have done well to have given into more often. Fanny, meanwhile, can only hope that she has made the right decision and that Sir Thomas will, in due course, feel "how wretched, and how unpardonable, how hopeless and how wicked it was, to marry without affection" (*MP* III.1.320). However, this takes a bit longer to penetrate – Sir Thomas persists in hoping that a personal approach by Henry might yet do the trick. It does at least mean that he decides to make no further attempt himself. He is gracious enough to say as much to Fanny: "You cannot suppose me capable of trying to persuade you to marry against your inclinations. Your happiness and advantage are all that I have in view" (*MP* III.2.326). This is all very well, but Fanny and the reader did indeed suppose this very thing during his rant to her about her refusal. Fanny herself makes allowances for what he does not know of the history and, particularly, of Henry's behaviour. Given that Sir Thomas had been happy for Maria to marry Mr Rushworth, "Romantic delicacy was certainly not to be expected from him" (*MP*

III.2.327). No, but a less brutal confrontation might, and also some respect for Fanny's personal wishes.

When the Crawfords leave the Grants, Sir Thomas hopes that Fanny will miss Henry, but he cannot make out what her reaction is: "She was always so gentle and retiring, that her emotions were beyond his discrimination" (*MP* III.6.362). Actually, most people's emotions are beyond his discrimination – that is his problem, and it becomes everyone else's problem. He misjudges the depth of Maria's emotion. He has no idea why everyone is afraid of him, but none of them (Edmund apart) really respects him. As far as Crawford is concerned, "[Sir Thomas] wished him to be a model of constancy; and fancied the best means of effecting it would be by not trying him too long" (*MP* III.4.341). He continues to hope. His next idea, following "one of his dignified musings" (*MP* III.6.364), is that Fanny should visit her family in Portsmouth. The real motive for this trip is that she should be confronted with the contrast between want and plenty and, as a result, think better of refusing a lifetime's expectation of plenty: "his prime motive in sending her away, had … nothing at all [to do] with any idea of making her happy … It was a medicinal project upon his niece's understanding, which he must consider as at present diseased" (*MP* III.6.365). This is typical of him. Sir Thomas expects Fanny to change her mind and marry a man she does not like merely because she experiences the chaotic and squalid life from which he has saved her. Fanny would sooner live in Portsmouth than with Henry Crawford. Sir Thomas manages with some difficulty to persuade Lady Bertram to part with her. It does not go down at all well, but "he was master at Mansfield Park. When he had really resolved on any measure, he could always carry it through" (*MP* III.6.366). Fanny's experience in Portsmouth does indeed cause her to contrast the chaos, noise and disorder of her father's house with life at Mansfield Park where "there would have been a consideration of times and seasons, a regulation of subject, a propriety, an attention towards every body which was not here" (*MP* III.7.378). Fanny feels the differences keenly, but it does not change her opinion of Henry, despite receiving a visit from him in Portsmouth.

In Fanny's absence, the seeds of disintegration, which were sown earlier, flourish at Mansfield Park. Tom's dissolute lifestyle catches up with him and he becomes very ill in London. He is removed to Mansfield Park and becomes worse. Mary Crawford begins to realise that if Tom dies, Edmund will become the only son. Then he will have to give up being a curate and in so doing will become a more attractive catch for her. This is a typical calculation on her part – she likes Edmund a lot, but never loses sight of the material benefits she would have to give up in marrying a relatively poor younger son. At the same time, Maria Rushworth has never got over her attraction to Henry. He joins her circle in Richmond and seduces her. She leaves her husband and throws in her lot with him. Her infidelity is more shocking than Lydia's elopement with Wickham in *Pride and Prejudice*. Maria Rushworth is married and rather older than Lydia. There are no financial considerations involved, like those that put pressure on Wickham to default on his debts. Henry seduces Maria because he can: it is a vanity project. But like Lydia, Maria believes that Crawford will marry her in the end. Unfortunately for Maria, no pressure can be brought to bear on Henry to marry against his inclination: Henry is already rich and cannot be bought off as Wickham is. He does not feel the shame of what he has done.

By the time Edmund writes to Fanny to confirm the news and invite her back, Julia has also eloped with Mr Yates, although in their case they marry. Julia's elopement is a reaction to Maria's: "her increased dread of her Father and of home ... imagining its certain consequence to herself would be greater severity and restraint – made her hastily resolve on avoiding such immediate horrors at all risks" (*MP* III.17.462). So she elopes to escape. The idea of regarding her father and her home with "dread" is just, well, dreadful. It drives her into accepting Yates, for whom she does not much care, as an available man who has stuck with her, and who is willing to marry her and take her away from her home. This is all Sir Thomas's doing. The Mansfield Park household reels under the successive shocks.

Fanny, on her return, is a comfort to Lady Bertram, who "did not think deeply, but, guided by Sir Thomas, she thought justly on all important points; and she saw, therefore, in all its enormity, what had happened, and neither endeavoured herself, nor required Fanny to advise her, to think little of guilt and infamy" (*MP* III.16.445). Here is a very explicit example of the father setting the moral standard. Sir Thomas's own situation must be worse: "There was but one of his children who was not at this time a source of misery to him" (*MP* III.16.447). Fanny realises that only Edmund has not, one way or another, been a disappointment to his father. From Sir Thomas's perspective, he is sorry even for Edmund, since Edmund's hopes of Mary Crawford must be finished following her brother's behaviour. In fact, Edmund is more miserable than even his father realises. He has been shocked by Mary's description of Maria's and Henry's behaviour: "no harsher name than folly given! – So voluntarily, so freely, so coolly to canvass it! – No reluctance, no horror, no feminine – shall I say? no modest loathings! – This is what the world does. For where, Fanny, shall we find a woman whom nature had so richly endowed? – Spoilt, spoilt!" (*MP* III.16.450–1). This is where you end up if you make jokes about rears and vices (see Chapter 6 of this book). Edmund's eyes are open at last to Mary's lack of worth, but his heart takes longer to accept what his intellect has recognised.

Had Sir Thomas better understood Mary Crawford's character, he would not have been so disappointed on Edmund's behalf. Sir Thomas, however, is doomed to misjudge all matters of character and emotion, and that is his tragedy. His inability to communicate his values and to show affection, his expectation that his children could be programmed like robots to behave well, regardless of their dispositions, his failure to penetrate any character, whether well known like Mrs Norris, or new like Henry Crawford – all his weaknesses have lost him the love and respect of those who should most have appreciated his many merits. It is a tragedy, which, like Admiral Crawford's disgraceful behaviour (see Chapter 6 of this book), is a form of contagion within his family. He is appalled and mortified at the outcomes for three of his children, and sad that Edmund should be disappointed in love. The children are the ones who have to deal with the fallout from his lack of judgement, his inability to excite their affection and respect, and his consequent failure to impart his moral standards.

In a long passage in Chapter 17 of Volume III, Austen reflects on Sir Thomas. "Sir Thomas, poor Sir Thomas, a parent, and conscious of errors in his own conduct as a parent, was the longest to suffer" (*MP* III.17.457). He has nothing but regrets, particularly of permitting Maria to marry Rushworth when he knew her heart was not in it. He gains some consolation over time. The Yates try very hard to atone for the elopement. Yates's financial position turns out not to be so bad and he is penitent. Tom, worn down by his illness and also remorseful about his part in the theatricals from which the original mischief had sprung, settles down into some steadiness. With respect to his daughters, Sir Thomas comes to realise that

> the excessive indulgence and flattery of their aunt had been continually contrasted with his own severity. He saw how ill he had judged, in expecting to counteract what was wrong in Mrs Norris, by its reverse in himself; clearly saw that he had but increased the evil, by teaching them to repress their spirits in his presence, as to make their real disposition unknown to him, and sending them for all their indulgences to a person who had been able to attach them only by the blindness of her affection, and the excess of her praise … He feared that principle, active principle, had been wanting, that they had never been properly taught to govern their inclinations and tempers, by that sense of duty which can alone suffice … Bitterly did he deplore a deficiency which now he could scarcely comprehend to have been possible. Wretchedly did he feel that with all the cost and care of an anxious and expensive education, he had brought up his daughters without their understanding their first duties, or his being acquainted with their character and temper. (*MP* III.17.459–60)

This is an unusually explicit summary of where a father has gone wrong. It shows Sir Thomas recognising and accepting his errors and responsibility. The reader does feel sorry for him. He simply did not have the emotional dimension necessary to build a constructive relationship with his children. At last he recognises the good in Fanny, and positively welcomes her engagement to Edmund:

> Sick of ambitious and mercenary connections, prizing more and more the sterling good of principle and temper, and chiefly anxious to bind by the strongest securities all that remained to him of domestic felicity, he had pondered with genuine satisfaction on the more than possibility of the two young friends finding their mutual consolation in each other for all that had occurred of disappointment to either; ... Fanny was indeed the daughter that he wanted. His charitable kindness had been rearing a prime comfort for himself. His liberality had a rich repayment, and the general goodness of his intentions by her, deserved it. He might have made her childhood happier; but it had been an error of judgment only which had given him the appearance of harshness, and deprived him of her early love; and now, on really knowing each other, their mutual attachment became very strong. (*MP* III.17.467–8)

So here is a novel in which the heroine is her own liberator. Sir Thomas finally recognises her worth. Edmund, kind to Fanny from the moment of her arrival at Mansfield Park, is too overwhelmed by Mary Crawford's charms to realise that Fanny is the only kindred spirit with whom he can look forward to lasting happiness. Edmund is no hero. There is no action taken on his part to overcome the difficulties presented by Sir Thomas's weaknesses and eventually bring them together. On the contrary, his infatuation with Mary Crawford creates a further obstacle to Fanny's happiness. While he has been her friend and protector within the family, his obsession with Mary Crawford leads him to gang up with the others to try to make Fanny take a part in the play. He, too, believed that she could be happy if she married Henry and encouraged her accordingly. He mopes after Mary Crawford long after any sensible man would have put her aside. It looks very much as if, when it comes to making judgements of other people, he is a chip off the old block. It is Fanny's determined stoicism in the face of Edmund's knuckle-headed regrets that quietly triumphs in the end. She waits patiently, just being herself, until he sees sense.

Sir Thomas does finally get rid of Mrs Norris from Mansfield Park. "He had felt her as an hourly evil, which was so much the worse, as there seemed no chance of its ceasing but with life; she seemed a part of himself, that must be borne forever" (*MP* III.17.461). Happily for him, Mrs Norris volunteers to be exiled with Maria in a distant establishment "shut up together with little society, on one side no affection, on the other, no judgment, it may be reasonably supposed that their tempers became their mutual punishment" (*MP* III.17.461). And so Sir Thomas achieves some sort of resolution within himself. Exiled and in seclusion, in effect locked up with Mrs Norris as his companion, it is Maria Rushworth who has paid most dearly for his failure.

Chapter 6
Orphans and Outsourcing

A number of the fathers who are important to the plotting of Austen's novels and with regard to the destiny of their children are either already dead by the time the novel opens or quickly die. These are: Darcy's father in *Pride and Prejudice*; Mr Thorpe, father of Isabella and John, in *Northanger Abbey*; and Henry Dashwood in *Sense and Sensibility*. They affect the plot in a number of ways: they have a critical impact on the behaviour or character of the child (Darcy); their absence leaves the children vulnerable to predators and/or to their own character weaknesses (Thorpe and Dashwood); or they leave their families in financial difficulty, which leads to material changes in their circumstances (Dashwood again).

The late Mr Darcy has a lot to answer for in relation to his son's faults and in letting Wickham believe that the Pemberley world owes him a living. Darcy sums up how the rest of the world viewed his behaviour before he reformed himself:

> As a child I was taught what was *right*, but I was not taught to correct my temper. I was given good principles, but left to follow them in pride and conceit. Unfortunately an only son, (for many years an only *child*) I was spoilt by my parents, who though good themselves, (my father particularly, all that was benevolent and amiable,) allowed, encouraged, almost taught me to be selfish and overbearing, to care for none beyond my own family circle, to think meanly of all the rest of the world, to *wish* at least to think meanly of their sense and worth compared with my own. Such I was, from eight to eight and twenty; and such I might still have been but for you, dearest, loveliest Elizabeth! (*PP* III.16.370)

Elizabeth had ruthlessly dismissed him for displaying these characteristics in his first proposal of marriage. It is only late in the novel that he realises how much of his faulty behaviour is attributable to his upbringing, although he does not expressly blame his father.

The cultivation of this behaviour means that he and Elizabeth have had more, and more interesting, hurdles to overcome than would have been the case if Darcy had been taught humility and self-control. But this is not the late Mr Darcy's only contribution to the plot. He was taken in by Wickham, and did not live to know the truth or see how Wickham abused his generosity. Wickham is charming and wicked in equal measure. Even Mr Bennet is described as "partial" (*PP* II.3.146) to him before he is unmasked. Wickham's expectations of indulgence from the Darcy family leads to no end of trouble, which is a good thing for the plot. Darcy fulfils his father's promises to Wickham by offering him the Church living and arranging for the purchase of his commission in the army when the living is declined. But Darcy can never shrug off this ill-judged legacy of his father's generosity. Not only does Wickham try to elope with Miss

Darcy for her fortune (£30,000; around £2 million today), he also turns up like a bad penny in Meryton and poisons Elizabeth's already rather negative opinion of Darcy's character. It gets worse – or rather, it gets better from the story's point of view: as a result of Darcy not wishing to get his hands dirty by advertising what he knows of Wickham's character, he ends up having to salvage a marriage between Wickham and Lydia Bennet, and ultimately becoming Wickham's brother-in-law. Elizabeth realises what a truly awful outcome this is for Darcy and understands how it could be the ruin of her recent new regard for Darcy: "Every kind of pride must revolt from the connection" (*PP* III.10.327). So Mr Darcy, for all he reveres his late father, has in fact been rather let down by him and by his failure to get Wickham's measure.

The Thorpe family in *Northanger Abbey* is a modest example of how children do not prosper when left in the hands of their indulgent mother, the father having died. The two eldest children, Isabella and John, are important characters in the Bath section of the book. The late Mr Thorpe was a lawyer in Putney and has left his family adequately, but not well, provided for. Catherine believes that Isabella has no fortune at all. Her lack of money will delay her marriage to James Morland, Catherine's brother. Disappointed, and perhaps mistaken about the Morland family wealth, she allows herself to fall for the attractive Captain Tilney, Henry's elder brother and heir to Northanger Abbey. Catherine expects them to get engaged, such is the appearance of their relationship, but Isabella's lack of fortune makes her unacceptable.

However, the late Mr Thorpe's relative lack of wealth is not the only, or worst, thing about his death. Mrs Thorpe is described as "a good humoured, well-meaning woman, and a very indulgent mother" (*NA* I.4.24). Red lights immediately flash on sight of the word "indulgent". Her son John has turned out a "rattle", a word which is out of use and which has no modern counterpart. It describes an inane and incessant, thoughtless chatterbox who displays foolish and noisy behaviour. (Perhaps it should be brought back into use.) Even the ingenuous Catherine is not misled; she finds John irritating from the outset. He, however, is unlikely to come to serious harm, though he may do it to others through his vain boasting. His eldest sister, Isabella, is very beautiful and a determined flirt. She is therefore likely to risk her respectability in running after the various men who take her fancy. She is positively predatory and flits capriciously from James Morland to Captain Tilney. She is shown tailing men who take her fancy through the streets of Bath.

It is no accident that these fatherless children behave badly, having no one to guide or restrain them and only an indulgent mother for company. When Catherine is cautioned by Mr Allen against gallivanting about the country with John Thorpe in an open carriage, she is concerned that Isabella ought to be alerted to the danger. Mr Allen is having none of this: "she is old enough to know what she is about; and if not, has a mother to advise her. Mrs Thorpe is too indulgent beyond a doubt" (*NA* I.13.95). Would Isabella's father have permitted it? Not likely. So she strays into and out of an engagement to the respectable James Morland, is attracted by the seductive Captain Richard Tilney, and cast off by him when he has finished amusing himself with her (to what extent, we do not know). Her future is uncertain and not likely to be happy.

Henry Dashwood is the most important of the dead fathers. He is alive right at the beginning of *Sense and Sensibility* for the purposes of explaining his complex financial situation, which boils down to the fact that the family's income depends on him staying alive. Unable to save up enough money before his death to leave his second wife and three daughters with any financial security, on his deathbed he asks his son from his first wife, John Dashwood, to look after them. These informal requests are very fragile (unless you are Darcy in *Pride and Prejudice* looking after Wickham in response to a request from your late father). Such promises were vague in nature, often given privately, and open to interpretation when it came to their implementation. John Dashwood and his wife Fanny are already amply provided for by his late mother and because Fanny has her own fortune. They nevertheless talk themselves out of doing anything at all for Mrs Dashwood and John's three half-sisters. Had they been honourable people, they would have made proper provision for the four women without having to be asked. As it is, they wriggle out of the informal promise through some splendid sophistry:

> [Fanny] did not at all approve of what her husband intended to do for his sisters. To take three thousand pounds from the fortune of their dear little boy, would be impoverishing him to the most dreadful degree ... related to him only by half blood, which she considered as no relationship at all ...
>
> 'It was my father's last request to me ... that I should assist his widow and daughters' ... 'ten to one but he was light headed at the time' ... 'it would be better for all parties if the sum were diminished one half' ... 'I may afford to give them five hundred pounds apiece' ... 'A hundred a year would make them all perfectly comfortable' ... 'I would not bind myself to allow them anything yearly' ... 'I am convinced within myself that your father had no idea of giving them any money at all' ... 'they will have five hundred a year amongst them, and

what on earth can four women want for more than that?
...

[John Dashwood] finally resolved, that it would be absolutely unnecessary, if not highly indecorous, to do more for the widow and children of his father, than such kind of neighbourly acts as his own wife pointed out. (*SS* I.2.8–13)

So now Mrs Dashwood, widow, and her three daughters are in a right pickle.

They must work out how they can live on the £7,000 Mr Dashwood has left his widow and the £1,000 that the uncle gives to each of the daughters. Not easily or well, is the answer. The income is £500 a year or about £35,000 for all four of them. They are by no means destitute, but it is a great comedown from the standard of living they enjoyed at Norland Park. Servants have to be dismissed. The carriage has to go. Economy and budgeting have to be considered for the first time. It becomes increasingly urgent that they find their own accommodation at a price they can afford. John Dashwood and his wife become every day less congenial as they take over occupation of Norland Park. Wondering where on earth she can go on her income, Mrs Dashwood is bailed out by a prosperous relation. Sir John Middleton offers them a cottage at a low rent near his home at Barton Park in Devon. Their modest income, supplemented by Sir John's hospitality and generosity, just about stretches to keep them respectably.

So the early death of Henry Dashwood and its financial consequences are the mainspring of the plot: robbing the Dashwood girls of any inheritance and forcing them out of their family home in Sussex into exile in Devonshire. They move from a stately home to a cottage. Henry Dashwood is not to be blamed entirely for this adverse turn of events. The uncle had intended to leave his substantial property outright to Henry Dashwood when he died. Unfortunately, this was converted late in the day to a life interest only. The change was brought about by the antics of John Dashwood's charming little boy. One wonders if the uncle would have changed his will for a charming little girl. Nor can Henry Dashwood be blamed for having died too soon to make alternative arrangements by way of saving, which he clearly intended to do. So this is not a particularly delinquent father, but one who has been thwarted by events beyond his control from fulfilling a father's basic duty to provide for his family. With the benefit of hindsight, his informal request to his son might have been discussed in the presence of both his own wife and his son's wife so that the fact of the promise and the extent of the assurance given by John Dashwood to carry it out would have been known more widely. Henry's widow and daughters are quite unaware of the fact that they have been cheated out of the comfortable living that John Dashwood could perfectly well have afforded to give them and which his father trusted him to do. Trusting to inheritors to behave well is a bit like expecting a hungry lion not to eat you. So Henry Dashwood is not entirely blameless on the financial front: he is naive. His absence, however, causes more mischief than a shortage of funds.

The forced move to Devonshire brings about various important events in the plot. The Middletons' neighbours include Colonel Brandon and also an elderly Mrs Smith whose heir apparent is Willoughby. These men become the rival suitors for Marianne Dashwood, the seventeen-year-old, beautiful and hopelessly romantic middle daughter. The Miss Steeles, the younger of whom is secretly engaged to Edward

Ferrars (enamoured of Elinor, the eldest Dashwood sister), are relatives of the Middletons. They are brought directly into the story when they are invited to stay at Barton Park.

Mrs Dashwood shares with Marianne a disposition to be romantic. With respect to her husband's death, her daughter Elinor "saw, with concern, the excess of her sister's sensibility; but by Mrs Dashwood it was valued and cherished. They encouraged each other now in the violence of their affliction. The agony of grief which overpowered them at first, was voluntarily renewed, was sought for, was created again and again" (*SS* I.1.7). In Chapter 12 of Volume I Mrs Dashwood is described as indulgent – that warning word again. Elinor shows her more temperate and level-headed approach by urging the disposal of an unwanted carriage and by cutting the number of servants they are to take to Devon. Here is another example in the novels of the heroine, or hero, trying to step in to steady the ship where the father is absent or negligent. Anne Elliot attempts it at the beginning of *Persuasion* in her seven-year plan of economies. Edmund Bertram tries to prevent the would-be thespians from putting on a play at *Mansfield Park*. Elizabeth Bennet pleads with her father not to let Lydia go to Brighton. They all fail, as they do not have the authority that only a father can bring to the problem at hand. Elinor Dashwood does succeed in reducing the expenses of the Barton cottage household. In emotional matters, however, she suffers serial failures in her attempts to get her mother to behave in a more considered and cautious manner with respect to Marianne and Willoughby. Her influence is just inadequate. A child cannot fill the vacuum left by the father. In particular, Elinor is unable to intervene in the saga of Marianne and Willoughby and establish whether or not they are actually engaged before serious damage is done.

While in Devon, Marianne and Willoughby fall in love, to the dismay of Colonel Brandon who is smitten with Marianne. They behave as if they are engaged. They hit it off straight away, with the approbation of Mrs Dashwood, who "entered into all their feelings with a warmth which left her no inclination for checking this excessive display of them. To her it was but the natural consequence of a strong affection in a young and ardent mind" (*SS* I.11.54). In due course, Willoughby is received at the cottage as if they are engaged. Mrs Dashwood encourages the relationship and does not see that there is any risk arising from there being no formal statement of engagement. She has no doubt of their being engaged, even after Willoughby leaves abruptly for London. When challenged by Elinor, she describes herself as:

> perfectly satisfied … his behaviour to Marianne and to all of us, for at least the last fortnight, declared that he loved her and considered her as his future wife … Has not my consent been daily asked by his looks, his manner, his attentive and affectionate respect? My Elinor, is it possible to doubt their engagement? How could such a thought occur to you? (*SS* I.15.79–80)

And much more besides. Elinor's uneasiness persists as the days pass with no word. She tries again to persuade her mother to ask Marianne if she is engaged to Willoughby. Her mother will have none of it, despite Marianne's young age. Elinor is not satisfied by the outcome: "common sense, common care, common prudence, were all sunk in Mrs Dashwood's romantic delicacy" (*SS* I.16.85). "Romantic delicacy" is a characteristic that is not fairly apportioned in Austen's work: Sir Thomas Bertram has none at all (see Chapter 5 of this book) when he might benefit from at least a bit, and Mrs Dashwood has so much that she fails to protect her daughter from the predatory, seductive Willoughby.

An engagement between Marianne and Willoughby becomes generally assumed beyond the immediate family. Colonel Brandon speaks of it as "very generally known" (*SS* II.5.167), and says that "their marriage is universally talked of" (*SS* II.5.168) by all their acquaintance. Elinor again applies to their mother to intervene, but she resists this request, still convinced of Willoughby's constancy. Of course, Mrs Dashwood turns out to be wrong. They were never engaged and Willoughby is short of money. Willoughby shuns the Dashwood sisters in London, ignoring Marianne's several letters. At a party where they are all present, he is forced to notice them, but makes only formal statements in response to Marianne's impassioned enquiry about whether or not he had received her notes: "'Yes, I had the pleasure of receiving the information of your arrival in town, which you were so good as to send me,' [he] turned hastily away ... Marianne, now looking dreadfully white, and unable to stand, sunk into her chair" (*SS* II.6.172). Marianne's behaviour is barely respectable as she tries to get him to account for his change of manner. He then becomes engaged to Miss Grey, or rather to her £50,000 (about £3.5 million today), and writes a formal, wounding letter to Marianne, returning her notes and a lock of her hair. Marianne's grief during these developments is boundless and would be described today as a nervous breakdown: [Elinor] "returned to Marianne, whom she found attempting to rise from the bed, and whom she reached just in time to prevent her from falling on the floor, faint and giddy from a long want of proper rest and food; for it was many days since she had any appetite, and many nights since she had really slept" (*SS* II.7.180). She goes on to neglect herself to the point of becoming dangerously ill.

The point here is that it is unimaginable that a concerned father would have permitted Marianne and Willoughby to carry on as if they were engaged without insisting that the man formally declare his position. A father, watchful of his seventeen-year-old daughter's interest, would have warded off the attentions of a young man who had not the means to fulfil the expectations that he was everywhere raising. The situation is actually worse than they know. Willoughby is a seducer and has already ruined the life of a young woman under Colonel Brandon's care by making her pregnant and then disappearing. No one has any suspicion of this until the Colonel tells Elinor, though not until the damage has been done, in Marianne's case. Her health and respectability are exposed as a result of a too-trusting mother, who cannot imagine that anyone so handsome, attractive, charming and romantic as Willoughby would jilt her daughter, never mind turn out to be a wicked seducer. Had Mr Dashwood been alive, the prolonged assumption that they were engaged would not have been permitted.

Marianne recovers her equilibrium eventually and marries the long-devoted Colonel Brandon, but this is as a result of a campaign by her family:

> [Mrs Dashwood's] wish of bringing Marianne and Colonel Brandon together ... was now her darling object ... and to see Marianne settled at the mansion-house was equally the wish of Edward and Elinor ... With such a confederacy against her – with a knowledge so intimate of his goodness – with a conviction of his fond attachment to herself, which at last, though long after it was

> observable to everybody else – burst on her – what could she do? (*SS* III.14.371)

So the hero in this case is Colonel Brandon, not Edward Ferrars. It is Brandon who resolves the problem of how Edward and Elinor are to have enough money to marry, and it is Brandon who assumes the care of Marianne. He has weathered early disappointment and tragedy in his life. Drawn to Marianne and hoping for a second chance at happiness, he has been stoical while she and Willoughby enjoyed their whirlwind romance. Elinor, too, has been heroic and stoical while Edward behaved oddly towards her and then turned out to be engaged to Lucy Steele. Brandon and Elinor are both rewarded for their resilience in the end.

Marianne's fate becomes a conventional one, but she is not the same person as she was before. Her particular susceptibility to the romantic, in which she was encouraged by her mother, and from which her father should have protected her, has been obliterated by illness and disappointment, perhaps also by depression. In assuming a very normal role "placed in a new home, a wife, the mistress of a family, and the patroness of a village" (*SS* III.14.371), the reader feels relieved that she has at last found some tranquillity, even if she has some regrets for the youthful romanticism that initially led her astray as a result of not being under a father's protection.

꙳

Several of the principal characters in the novels are brought up by relatives who are not their parents, usually uncles and aunts. This is not always because their natural parents are dead. In *Emma*, Frank Churchill, né Weston, is brought up from a very young age by his late mother's brother and his wife. Frank's father, Mr Weston, is alive and remarries Miss Taylor as the novel opens. He had voluntarily handed over his son to the Churchills. In *Mansfield Park*, Fanny Price is brought up by Sir Thomas and Lady Bertram (Lady Bertram being her mother's sister), although both Fanny's parents are alive. Like Mr Weston, they too voluntarily hand over a child. In *Mansfield Park*, Mary and Henry Crawford, who are orphans, are brought up by their uncle, Admiral Crawford, and his wife Mrs Crawford (until her death). The reader knows nothing of the Crawford parents.

Of the characters who stand in as parents, Sir Thomas Bertram has four children of his own, and becomes Fanny Price's guardian. He is a major character and is dealt with in Chapter 5 of this book. The others are stand-in parents and childless. They are the Churchills, and Admiral and Mrs Croft. Also dealt with below is Mr Price, father to Fanny. The Churchills are off stage, although the disposition of Mrs Churchill is amply reported and important to the plot. Admiral Croft is also only reported, but his upbringing of Henry and Mary is important and he also plays a role in the promotion of William Price, Fanny's eldest brother.

In *Emma*, Mr Weston's first wife dies when Frank is very young. Mr Weston hands him over to be brought up by his in-laws, the wealthy and childless Churchills. Mr Weston is treated sympathetically by Austen, described as having a "warm heart and sweet temper" (*E* I.2.13). The circumstances were difficult for him, as his marriage caused a breach with his wife's wealthy family. The first Mrs Weston was never truly reconciled to having to give up the comforts of her family's wealth for her husband's poorer circumstances. They overspent as a result. So Mr Weston is in the category of having chosen his first wife badly. Her death leaves him financially straitened and with a small son:

> The boy had, with the additional softening claim of a lingering illness of his mother's, been the means of a sort of reconciliation; and Mr and Mrs Churchill ... offered to take the whole charge of the little Frank soon after her decease ... the child was given up to the care and the wealth of the Churchills, and [Mr Weston] had only his own comfort to seek and his own situation to improve as he could. (*E* I.2.14)

Frank takes the Churchill name. He will be their heir. In the meantime, Mr Weston prospers and eventually takes a second wife in the form of Miss Taylor, Emma's former governess, still living with the Woodhouses as Emma's companion when Mr Weston proposes to her. In the course of the book Mrs Weston gives birth to a daughter.

Austen does not openly criticise Mr Weston for having handed over his son in these circumstances, although it was clearly not ideal that he should have married a woman who was not committed to live within her reduced means. Her death was obviously unlooked for. The prospects for Frank, practical and financial, were much better with the Churchills than his father could have offered. Mr Weston is proud of his son, seeing him every year and looking forward to showing him off in Highbury when Frank visits his father on the occasion of his marriage to Miss Taylor. Not everyone approves of Mr Weston's decision to part with his son. Mrs John Knightley, sister to Emma and an indulgent mother, cannot conceive of parting with a child, but her husband John, marked out in the novel as an acute observer of life and a reliable judge of others, puts a different gloss on it: "Mr Weston is rather an easy, cheerful tempered man, than a man of strong feelings; he takes things as he finds them, ... depending ... much more upon what is called *society* for his comforts ... than upon family affection, or any thing that home affords" (*E* I.11.95). John Knightley is likely intended to be understood as being near the mark, although this lukewarm assessment of Mr Weston does not suit Emma's more partial view. The main point is that the inability and/or disinclination of Mr Weston to bring up his own son have important consequences for the plot.

The first is that Frank has expectations of the Churchills, which are significant. With those expectations come obligations. A rift with them is unthinkable for a man whose expectations from his father are nil, especially since the father has remarried, will father other children, and has assumed that Frank will not look to him for money. Frank simply cannot afford to upset them. This is unfortunate because the second issue is the character of the aunt. Mrs Churchill is said to be a "capricious woman [who] governed her husband entirely" (*E* I 2.15). She has to be appeased. Her whims have to be gratified. Her fancies (or so they are thought) about her health have to be respected. This has negative consequences for Frank. He is at her beck and call.

Mrs Churchill is selfish and demanding, and clearly has no real regard for Frank's interests. She expects that he will marry well, that is, to money. This status-driven woman, who has already broken with Frank's mother over her marriage to Mr Weston, delivers a similar message to Frank and his generation: he cannot marry where he chooses, despite having the prospect of significant wealth, without the risk of forfeiting the Churchills' protection and finance. As a result, his engagement to Jane Fairfax, who is penniless, has to be concealed. This causes mischief for Emma, as Frank flirts with her to divert attention from Jane, feeding his father's and Mrs Weston's hopes of an attachment between them. Such deception would not have been necessary in his father's house, but Frank trades principle for romance, profit and advantage, without calculating or caring about the risk either to Jane's respectability or to Emma's feelings.

His upbringing has given him an unfortunate degree of selfishness that all his charm and good looks cannot quite dispel. When the secret engagement is revealed, Emma calls it "a very abominable sort of proceeding … a system of hypocrisy and deceit, – espionage, and treachery? – To come among us with professions of openness and simplicity; and such a league in secret to judge us all!" (*E* III.10.393). This being a comedy, no harm and much good are done at the end, especially since Frank's artificial dalliance with Emma makes Mr Knightley jealous (not always a negative emotion in the novels – think Anne Elliot and Captain Wentworth, Fanny Price, Colonel Brandon). The concealed engagement is an important part of the plot, as Emma and the reader are led up and down all sorts of garden paths before the true position is revealed late in the day. Clues are everywhere strewn around (the timing of Frank's arrival, the haircut, the piano, the spectacle repair), but not picked up.

In order to resolve the impasse of Mrs Churchill's opposition to Frank's marriage to a woman of no means, Austen has to kill her off. Mr Weston, despite being the natural father, has no role or influence in the matter. But it was his decision to pass Frank on to the Churchills which resulted in the need for secrecy in the first place.

Mr Price in *Mansfield Park* is the other father in Austen's novels who gives away a child. He is described as a "Lieutenant of Marines, without education, fortune or connections" (*MP* I.1.3). He is one of only two naval characters whom the reader does not admire, the other being Admiral Crawford, also in *Mansfield Park* (Jane Austen's own family connections to the navy ensure that they generally get a good press in her books). Sir Thomas Bertram, the prosperous brother-in-law, might have helped out the Price family earlier but for a quarrel between Mrs Price, on the one hand, and her two sisters, Lady Bertram and Mrs Norris, on the other. Mr Price is "an husband disabled for active service, but not the less equal to company and good liquor, and a very small income to supply their wants" (*MP* I.1.4). While awaiting their ninth child, the mother looks at last to patch up relations with her more prosperous sister and place a child with her; she sends Fanny.

Having kicked off the story by describing how Mr Price's indigence results in the family needing to part with Fanny, the reader has to wait until she is sent by Sir Thomas Bertram to Portsmouth for a reunion in Chapter 7 of Volume III before more is known of their domestic distresses. The house is disorderly and her father worse than Fanny had expected:

> more negligent of his family … manners coarser … He did not want abilities; but he had no curiosity and no information beyond his profession; he read only the newspaper and the navy-list; he talked only of the dockyard, the harbour, Spithead, and the Motherbank; he swore and he drank, he was dirty and gross … She had never been able to recal anything approaching to tenderness in his former treatment of herself. There had remained only a general impression of roughness and loudness; and now he scarcely ever noticed her, but to make her the object of a coarse joke. (*MP* III.8.385)

This is a highly unpleasant description. The only consolation is that he is shown as not physically violent. He can also appear to some advantage when he chooses. When Henry Crawford turns up unannounced to visit Fanny in Portsmouth, they meet her father by chance. He tries to make a good impression: "His manners now, though not polished, were more than passable; they were grateful, animated, manly; his expressions were those of an attached father, and a sensible man; – his loud tones did very well in the open air, and there was not a single oath to be heard" (*MP* III.10.398).

Mr Price is, then, something of a Jekyll and Hyde, with Hyde very much to the fore in his natural state and Jekyll appearing only when he thinks the circumstances merit it. But he can effect the change if he makes an effort; he just never normally makes an effort. Austen makes no explicit comment on the relationship between this self-indulgent, financially imprudent and careless man and his large number of children. She is not against large families – the approved Mr Morland in *Northanger Abbey* has ten of them, but he can afford it. Austen clearly disapproves of marrying or having children if the means are not there to support them properly. In the late eighteenth and early nineteenth centuries, the government did not provide any form of subsidy. If the father could not provide the money to raise his children decently, then the family had no business having children in the first place. There is a clear implication that the Prices should have limited the size of their family. Mr Price cannot provide for a large family, but he has one anyway. It is Mr Price's refusal to think about this that is the trigger for the initial part of the plot: Fanny's removal to Mansfield Park to be brought up by her aunt and uncle. A father who had more care for his family would not have so badly mismatched his income and liabilities that his wife has to heal a breach with her sisters in order to give away one of her children. So here we have an instance of a father whose indigence is the main reason for the heroine's fate, namely, of being brought up at Mansfield Park instead of in her own home. This turns out well for Fanny in the end, but she has much misery to endure before the happy ending.

The Crawfords, sister and brother, are a wonderfully engaging pair, but tragic in their destinies despite their wealth. Mary has £20,000 (getting on for £1.5m today) and Henry has an estate in Norfolk – the implication is he has more. It all goes wrong for them when their parents die and they are brought up by Admiral and Mrs Crawford, their uncle and his wife. The Admiral takes a close interest in Henry, while his wife focuses on Mary. In his role as the father figure, Admiral Croft damages the characters of both his niece and nephew. Given the importance of Mary and Henry for, respectively, Edmund Bertram and Fanny Price, the Admiral may be a minor character who occupies a modest amount of text and whose actions are only reported, but he is an influential one.

While Admiral Crawford's wife was alive, both brother and sister lived with their aunt and uncle. Upon the aunt's death, the Admiral's behaviour prompts Mary to leave his house. Mary finds it expedient to move because the Admiral was, as Austen puts it, "a man of vicious conduct, who chose, instead of retaining his niece, to bring his mistress under his own roof" (*MP* I.4.40). "Vicious" is an extreme word. This is racy stuff for Austen in a novel that has more than its fair share of racy behaviour and sexual licence. Mary takes up residence with her sister, Mrs Grant. Mrs Grant is the wife of the clergyman who assumes the living at Mansfield Park on the death of Mr Norris. In this way, the Admiral's immoral behaviour results in

Henry and Mary becoming neighbours of the family at Mansfield Park.

Mary Crawford reveals that she deplores the impact the Admiral has had on her brother when they discuss Henry's intention to marry Fanny. Henry realises there is no point in discussing his intentions with his uncle because the Admiral hated marriage "and thought it never pardonable in a young man of independent fortune" (*MP* II. 12.287). So if you do not need to marry for money, better not to marry at all, but to acquire sexual pleasure by seduction or purchase. Indeed, this is the principle by which Henry conducts himself. Mary, on the other hand, regards Henry's marriage to Fanny as a means of rescuing her brother from the evil influence of the uncle. She feels strongly about it:

> the advantage to you of getting away from the Admiral before your manners are hurt by the contagion of his, before you have contracted any of his foolish opinions, or learnt to sit over your dinner, as if it were the best blessing of life! – *You* are not sensible of the gain, for your regard for him has blinded you; but in my estimation your marrying early may be the saving of you. To have seen you grow like the Admiral in word or deed, look or gesture, would have broke my heart. (*MP* II. 12.290–1)

Henry thinks her reaction too strong and describes his uncle as a good man, despite his faults: "more than a father to me. Few fathers would have let me have my own way half so much" (*MP* II.12.291). Quite so. A father should have been a restraining influence for the benefit of his son's moral well-being. In Chapter 5 of this book I have shown how, in the same novel, Sir Thomas Bertram seeks to tame his elder son Tom's wild behaviour. He fails until a serious illness intervenes to bring Tom to his senses. In Henry's case, his uncle is making efforts to encourage him in immoral habits and he succeeds. Henry's wish is that, as far as the Admiral is concerned, his sister Mary "must not prejudice Fanny against him. I must have them love one another" (*MP* II.12.291). The idea that Fanny could ever love a man who has driven out his niece as a result of installing his mistress is laughable. It shows how Henry has completely misjudged her moral calibre and how she would react to a man who lived openly with his mistress.

Henry's self-indulgence and selfishness have been encouraged, rather than curbed, by the Admiral, leading to Henry's capricious behaviour towards women, who are evidently susceptible to his particular brand of charm. Quite what this consists of is mysterious, since he is not in the conventional category of tall and handsome. Perhaps his strongly self-centred character radiates a confidence that women find a very attractive challenge. Henry thinks nothing of leading on both the Bertram sisters. He then plots to make Fanny fall for him; but she is already committed to Edmund, and in any event, has formed a very poor opinion of Henry as a result of his behaviour towards Maria and Julia. Thwarted in what started out as a game to pass the time, Henry suddenly finds himself unexpectedly and genuinely in love. It now becomes a serious matter to get Fanny to love him back. He cannot achieve it because the distractions of Maria Rushworth in London and Richmond prove too much for him. Fanny is saved, but Henry is lost, taking Maria with him.

Admiral Crawford's malign influence is much greater than Mary asserts or suspects. It extends to her own lack of principle, and her lack of regard for, or even appreciation of, principle in others. Edmund eventually recognises this when he hears her reaction to Maria's elopement with Henry (see

Chapter 5 of this book). This is evidence he cannot ignore, but it comes late in the novel after Edmund has overlooked many examples of Mary's failings. There have, by this time, been numerous other occasions when he regretted her lack of delicacy or empathy with his wish to be a clergyman. He just finds excuses for her. It is plain early on that exposure to the Admiral has coarsened Mary's manners. In discussing admirals as a class, Mary jokes with Edmund, "my home at my uncle's brought me acquainted with a circle of admirals. Of *Rears*, and *Vices*, I saw enough. Now do not be suspecting me of a pun, I entreat" (*MP* I.6.60). More racy stuff. Edmund's response to this most unladylike sally is merely to be grave. Edmund leads a see-saw emotional life as Mary veers between sincerity, well-meant feeling and vulgarity. She is at her best when behaving protectively towards Fanny, such as when Fanny is distressed by the others bullying her. In the end, it will not do. Her exposure to the morals of her uncle has damaged her beyond repair, making her unfit to appreciate the good qualities of Edmund's character. Fanny is disgusted: "The woman who could speak of him, and speak only of his appearance! – What an unworthy attachment!" (*MP* III.12.413). Mary prefers material advantage and a house in London to the quiet seclusion of a country parsonage, even if it is inhabited by Edmund.

One way or another, Austen sees the vices of Admiral Crawford as having malformed the characters of his niece and nephew. Much of the plot turns on their destiny and their effect on Edmund and Fanny. Had Admiral Crawford observed proper moral principles himself and educated them in principled behaviour, as a good father would have done, then they would never have had occasion to leave his house and come to Mansfield Park. It is the Admiral's immoral behaviour that displaces Mary to the Grants at Mansfield Park and throws her and her brother in the way of the Bertrams and Fanny. If they had met at Mansfield Park, untainted by Admiral Crawford's "vicious conduct", it is probable that Edmund would have married Mary, and Fanny married Henry. On occasion, the Crawford siblings show a capacity for goodness which indicates that, brought up differently, they would have earned Austen's ultimate accolade: respectability. They are clever, attractive, wealthy, and have lively and engaging dispositions. As it is, their acquired "father" has warped their characters beyond repair. This is tragic for both of them. It is difficult to believe that either of them will find happiness, despite the advantages to which they were born. Mary suffers for it:

> Mary, though perfectly resolved against ever attaching herself to a younger brother again, was long in finding among the dashing representatives, or idle heir apparents, who were at the command of her beauty and her [£20,000] any one who could satisfy the better taste she had acquired at Mansfield, whose character and manners could authorise a hope of the domestic happiness she had there learnt to estimate, or put Edmund Bertram sufficiently out of her head. (*MP* III.17.465)

So she ends up in moral purgatory: sufficiently enlightened to wish herself married to an Edmund, but not reformed enough to get one. There is always at least one woman left by the wayside at the end of Austen's novels. In *Mansfield Park* there are two: Mary Crawford and Maria Bertram.

Conclusion

Austen's recipe for successful fatherhood is: be very careful in the selection of your wife; keep within your income; plan for your demise; if you have money, use it for the children's education and welfare, but do not on any account indulge them; teach them your values; and control any tendency they may have to despise or treat others badly or rudely; be affectionate towards them; praise their efforts and encourage greater achievement; be careful of the company they keep; make sure they do not marry for the wrong reasons or on too little money; do not allow them to be motivated by money beyond being sensible about what they will need to live on; hold out against the children's wishes if their long-term interests are at stake.

The destructiveness of the principal fathers, namely, Bennet, Woodhouse, Tilney, Dashwood, Elliot and Bertram, is not allowed to blight all lives, but it is a close-run thing, as shown by the following assessment of how they measure up against the three broad standards of financial security, education and happiness.

Mr Bennet fails on all counts as a father. He chooses a very silly wife, whom he insults. He spends all his money without making provision for his family in the event of his death, when they will be evicted by Mr Collins. The absence of a financial safety net is entirely his own choice. He neglects his daughters' education: it is self-service if they have the inclination, which mostly they do not. Even if they do, their self-education is random and of doubtful quality. In this respect Elizabeth recognises that she is outgunned by the Bingley sisters. The family's manners in public (Jane and Elizabeth apart) are presumptuous and vulgar. Mr Bennet neither establishes, nor maintains, standards of good and respectable behaviour. He will not confront or control impropriety. He is passive, almost reclusive, in his library. Emerging for social occasions, his only amusement is to make fun of his family and friends. Exertion is unknown to him. He shows no interest in his daughters' welfare or happiness, not caring if they are jilted, disappointed in love, shamed, or mortified (in public *or* private). He makes jokes at their expense. His inertia results in the worst disgrace for Lydia (sex without marriage), a stigma that attaches to the whole family. His neglect of Lydia is so complete that she does not even realise the enormity of what she has done.

Mr Bennet does not wipe his whole family from the face of respectable society: he is rescued by Darcy as part of Darcy's own rehabilitation. Darcy is remorseful because his pride prevented him from showing Wickham up for what he was. Armed by his love for Elizabeth and by his zeal to put right his mistake, Darcy sweeps in to London to deal with Wickham and Lydia. He confronts the miscreants and puts up the money to make them marry. With the Wickhams now made respectable, even if a little late in the day, Darcy goes on to approve of Bingley resuming his courtship of Jane Bennet. He follows Bingley's lead by trying his luck once more with Elizabeth. If Mr Bennet had not been so neglectful of his duties, none of this would have been necessary. The sense of urgency to marry well in case Mr Bennet should die, the repulsive manners of the mother and younger daughters, the disgrace of Lydia – all derive from Mr Bennet's failure as a father.

In *Emma*, Mr Woodhouse gets the money right, although it costs him no effort – he has lots of it without him having to lift a finger. Emma is never going to be destitute. He fails on all other fronts. Mr Woodhouse has provided for Emma's education, but not for her to perform to the level of her considerable abilities. No one has kept her nose to the grindstone. She has been praised, but not criticised. She has never had to exert herself and has therefore never excelled. She has a very high opinion of herself as a result of being adored and complimented by her father and Miss Taylor (although not by Mr Knightley), and she starts meddling in other people's affairs. Mr Woodhouse idolises Emma, but only so long as she stays exactly as she is: running after his every whim, remaining unmarried and devoted exclusively to him. He is like a demanding god set in a lofty temple with Emma as the sole votary. He has no space in his very small brain for her happiness, welfare and future. He cannot even have a proper conversation with her. If he thinks about it at all, he sees her as completely fulfilled in looking after him and cannot imagine why she would wish to do anything else. He becomes increasingly dependent on her, resenting her going anywhere. His every comfort depends on her forethought and planning.

If there is the smallest wrinkle in his convenience, he sets up as noisy and effective a wail as any baby. He has her absolutely where he wants her and has not the slightest intention of letting her go.

Mr Knightley is very appropriately named. He rides to the rescue from next door. He is likely the only man on the planet who is prepared to live with a father-in-law like Mr Woodhouse. This is the way to square Emma's determination to tend to her father's needs with Mr Knightley's desire to marry her. He is the only man who could become her husband. Mr Knightley also counteracts everyone else's tendency to see no fault in Emma. He sets standards and provides guidance to correct her, playing the role of mentor, which her father could not do. His age at thirty-seven is important – as he keeps pointing out to her, he has more than a head start in experience and judgement. She exerts herself to do better to please him and deserve his praise. He takes on some of the burden of amusing Mr Woodhouse. In due course, the reader hopes that Knightley children will provide a healthy distraction from Mr Woodhouse. Eventually, as the nineteenth-century Italian writer Lampedusa pointed out, while there's death, there's hope. Just as with Mrs Churchill, some ailment or other will prove real rather than imaginary, and Mr Woodhouse will at last go the way of all flesh.

In *Northanger Abbey*, General Tilney, like Mr Woodhouse, is very rich; no child of his will ever know what it is to be in need of money. Also like Mr Woodhouse, he has lost his wife to an early death, so his temper rules the household. He has a very different temperament from Mr Woodhouse. He is demanding, but in a much more assertive way. Instead of sitting around and expecting attention, he strides around and gives orders. He has provided for his children's education; they are well read and charming – or at least Henry and Isabella are – but he treats his children as if they are objects. Despite his wealth, he has no wish to use it to further their happiness if they wish to marry someone who is poor but otherwise suitable. His intention is to use his children to add to the family wealth. He has no regard for their feelings, assuming he thinks they have any. He has already stood in the way of Eleanor marrying a man who is nice but poor. He has ordered Henry to become attached to Catherine when he thinks she is rich, and ordered him to become detached from her when he realises she is not. When Henry refuses to obey, he throws a hissy fit and refuses to speak to him. He also refuses to consent to the marriage even though Henry has enough money of his own not to need any from his father. Both children are prisoners of his attitude. They either obey or they are non-persons. He behaves like an absolute tyrant and is by a mile the most unpleasant of all the fathers (although my vote still goes to Mrs Norris in *Mansfield Park* as the most unpleasant character).

The rescue in this case (as for Frank Churchill and Jane Fairfax in *Emma*) comes in the form of a lucky death. Eleanor's suitor converts, like Superman in a telephone box, from a poor commoner to a rich viscount. General Tilney is still not the slightest bit interested in whether he is suitable as Eleanor's husband now that he is rich and titled compared to when he was poor and ordinary. Money and status are all that matter to him. So she marries and escapes from Northanger Abbey. In light of his daughter's coup, General Tilney is eventually persuaded to give way over Henry and Catherine.

In *Sense and Sensibility*, the late Henry Dashwood has left his family without a roof over their heads and with just about enough income to save them from want. So nul points on the financial front. The daughters will have to marry some money if they are to marry at all. They are cast into exile in Devonshire where the plot develops. The late Mr Dashwood does seem to have done quite well on the educational front, as both elder sisters seem talented and well read, although Marianne could show more patience and forbearance with those who are not her cup of tea. But his death means that he cannot counteract his wife's and Marianne's disposition to hopeless romanticism. This leaves Marianne unprotected, particularly from the handsome, dashing, sexually magnetic and completely unscrupulous Willoughby. He may well have been truly in love with Marianne, but money talks, and his lack of it drives him into a hasty marriage with another. Marianne's nervous collapse after he jilts her takes an awful toll on her health and curtails her previously exuberant spirits. It fits her to marry Colonel Brandon, who is devoted to her, but she has undergone a personality change. Colonel Brandon is the true deliverer and hero in *Sense and Sensibility*, not Edward Ferrars, Elinor's suitor. Colonel Brandon continues to court Marianne after Willoughby has cast her off. He provides the income that enables Elinor to marry Edward Ferrars after Lucy Steele has taken off with Edward's brother. Like Mr Knightley in *Emma*, he is over thirty-five and steps into a paternal role as protector and provider for the Dashwood sisters in place of the late Mr Dashwood.

In *Persuasion*, Sir Walter Elliot has carelessly run out of money and into debt, with the result that he has to rent out his home and live more cheaply elsewhere. His indebtedness also means that his daughters have to marry where there is money. As with Mr Bennet, this penury was entirely avoidable, if only he had shown some self-control in his spending. So he is another financial failure. Clearly a stupid man, he does not score well either on education or his personal relations with his children. Anne is a pianist of some skill, and Lady Russell seems to have been helpful in overseeing her upbringing. Elizabeth is as cloth-headed as her father and equally disdainful of those around her. She has likely never read a book in her life. Sir Walter is also a hopeless custodian of his daughters' welfare. He is not very pleased with Mary's marriage to Charles Musgrove because Charles has no rank. The fact that he had enough money, with the prospect of inheriting more, seems to have been lost on Sir Walter. He positively refuses to countenance Anne's engagement to Captain Wentworth when it is first proposed. He is converted to the cause only because he has little time for Anne and it is clear to him that Captain Wentworth is handsome, and later, both rich and distinguished. As with Charles Musgrove, he thinks that the Captain is gaining more than he is giving. And as for Elizabeth, her shared value for rank even over wealth will likely leave her a spinster and vulnerable when her father dies. Her father does not seem anxious about it as he should. She has to hope that he lives long enough without marrying to repair the family fortunes.

In *Mansfield Park*, Sir Thomas Bertram so nearly gets it right. It is his tragedy that he misjudges the upbringing of his children so that Maria comes to a bad end, and Julia and Tom come close to it. He does quite well financially, but fails to curb Tom's tendency to run up substantial debts. Overall, he has wealth enough to look after his family and he is careful about it, failing only to make Tom behave prudently. He has tried hard with education, again not quite managing to achieve what he wanted. He insists on discipline, but fails to instil values. Having married an indolent wife, he trusts too much to his sister-in-law, Mrs Norris, who proves to be destructive. He is a poor judge of character. He has shades of both Tilney and Elliot in valuing rank and wealth above character, making a weak challenge to the Rushworth marriage and risking Fanny's happiness by putting pressure on her to marry Crawford. He reaps a bitter harvest. Tom is brought to death's door by his dissolute life; Maria abandons her husband for Crawford, and is then cast off by him and exiled with Mrs Norris; Julia elopes with the flaky Yates to escape her father's wrath when news breaks of Maria's elopement; Edmund misjudges Mary Crawford's worth and nurses his wounds by sitting with Fanny. In this case, it is the heroine Fanny who has shown steadfast principle throughout; she has had the resilience to resist Crawford and to wait for Edmund to come to realise that he loves her. She rescues what is left of Sir Thomas's happiness. Tom recovers and shows promise that he will behave prudently. The Yates may yet make a go of it. It is Fanny and Edmund who provide certainty of happiness, and Sir Thomas can only be grateful for the part he has played in that.

༄༅

The intention of this book has been to show that the heroines of Austen's novels are caught in a trap made by their fathers' failure to observe the three basic parental duties: financial security, education and happiness. Austen also shows that getting it wrong takes a great variety of forms. Intervention can be as damaging as doing nothing. General Tilney in *Northanger Abbey* is a control freak, Sir Thomas Bertram in *Mansfield Park* has tendencies in the same direction, Mr Bennet in *Pride and Prejudice* could not be more hands off, Sir Walter Elliot in

Persuasion is interested only in himself, as is Mr Woodhouse in *Emma*. Their common weakness is the lack of an emotional connection to their children, especially to their daughters. Their differences of character, temper, behaviour and demeanour would not matter one jot if they were emotionally sympathetic to the daughters' interests and were prepared to exert themselves unselfishly for their daughters' benefit. This is why Austen's portraits of failed fathers still resonate today. The social context is different, but the issue is the same: these fathers fail because in their hearts they do not connect. This is why Sir Thomas is a truly tragic figure and one reason why *Mansfield Park* is such a great novel. He tries hard. He means well. He really intends that his children and Fanny should flourish. By the end of the book he is close to being a broken man. Only through Fanny is he redeemed, restored to equilibrium with a better knowledge of himself.

But Austen is not gloomy about fathers, despite her focus on their failures. She does not believe that children are inescapably prisoners of the parents' inheritance. She does demonstrate that redemption is possible for the daughters, if not their fathers. The heroines accomplish it through their own stoicism and innate sense of principle. Emma Woodhouse, Elizabeth Bennet, Elinor Dashwood and Catherine Morland have heroes to help them. Anne Elliot and, especially, Fanny Price have to find all the resources within themselves. So, finally, spare a thought for those who do not live happily ever after as they had hoped and expected: Marianne in *Sense and Sensibility* puts up with second best in Colonel Brandon, and the Crawfords in *Mansfield Park* will be in the same boat; Maria Rushworth is banished from Mansfield Park and locked up with Mrs Norris; Elizabeth Elliot in *Persuasion* stays firmly on the shelf; Lydia Bennet has a very uneven relationship with her Wickham. All of them have been let down by their fathers, but they are the ones who will live with the consequences.

Made in the USA
Charleston, SC
20 March 2015